Praise for *Love: A Guide t*

MW00791638

Early in LOVE: A Guide to Life Partnering, *the newest addition to their Messy Marvelous series, Montanez and Merck warn that "love is not enough," which, in the hands of less skilled therapists, is a gut-shot declaration with the potential to inspire fear and trepidation. Instead, these co-authors—in crystal-clear prose that is simultaneously conversational and confident—provide a toolbox chock full of skills to negotiate the often bumpy, always changing topography of a loving relationship. Using a guiding metaphor of building a house, Merck and Montanez tell us how to create the blueprints for healthy, lasting relationships, then how to construct our relationships so they evolve and thrive and endure. Trust me, this is a book written for the real world, for real people who desire real relationships. And it is not a book designed to be a once-over; you'll find yourself returning again and again to dog-eared pages for pragmatic direction. (Confession: I've already printed out the "8 ULTRAS" and taped them to my computer.) The twenty skills Montanez and Merck outline in* LOVE *have the power to transform the many mazes of a relationship into clear-cut, attainable, desirable destinations.*

> —Scott Gould, author of *Whereabouts* and *Things That Crash, Things That Fly*

As Amy Sander Montanez and Rhea Ann Merck thoroughly demonstrate in their practical guide to love, when we enter an intimate relationship we must wrestle with profound questions, including, "Who are you?" and, "Who am I?" Finding creative solutions to the challenges of coupledom requires a willingness to risk being hurt in the pursuit of one of life's most meaningful journeys. By supplying mental exercises, often humorous real-life examples, and a wide range of additional resources, Merck and Montanez are expert guides to the messy, marvelous world of deep commitment.

> —Mark Leviton, *The Sun Magazine*

Praise for *Love: A Guide to Life Partnering*

This book is an essential guide to all-things-relationships. Amy and Rhea distill decades of experience working with couples, as well as their personal wisdom, into 20 actionable relationship skills—from "building trust" to "learning to fight." Each chapter contains engaging anecdotes, thought-provoking questions, practical exercises, and links to additional resources. Whether currently in or out of a relationship, readers will take away valuable tools that they can use right off the page.

—Talia Litman, MFT, marriage and family therapist, and author specializing in couples and sex therapy [Contact: taliamft.com]

In my work with engaged couples I'm often asked, "what is the secret to a healthy marriage?" And although there is no "secret," there is this truism: Healthy couples do the things that unhealthy couples avoid. Period. That's it. Read this book. Build your marriage. Don't wait for the hurricane to come before you say to each other, "I guess we need a roof." Amy and Rhea have provided an artful way to navigate the laboratory of family systems that make each marriage unique and altogether the same, two people doing life together in messy marvelous love.

—Rev. Kevin M. Roberts, Principal and Practitioner, VOW Marriage Planning [vownashville.com]

Amy and Rhea are back with more great wisdom, stories, and practical life skills that make romantic relationships work! As someone who's been married for 22 years, I admit there were some skills mentioned I need to sharpen. These make for great discussions too! This book is a great resource and conversation tool. I'll be referring friends and clients to it often.

—April Pertuis, creator, writer, and founder of *Lightbeamers* and *The Inside Story Podcast* [Contact: lightbeamers.com]

Praise for *Love: A Guide to Life Partnering*

I thought that as a priest who has seen a share of the messiness and marvelousness of the world, I would have "building a successful and fulfilling relationship" reasonably figured out. It's all about communication, right? LOVE made me pause and dig deep into myself and our relationship. Love isn't something that can be built out of the box like an IKEA shelf. Amy and Rhea give you the blueprints and the list of tools you need to build a house that will stand, with all the warmth and good advice you'd expect from a good friend over a cup of tea. Their sincere and tender writing, laced with personal storytelling, lowers your defenses and opens you up to the deepness that building love with someone holds. It's as if they take your hand and say, "We've walked this trail before and know the way. Come on, let's go together." I'm grateful to have read this book and I know that my fiancé and I will be exploring these chapters again and again as our lives bloom together.

—The Reverend Caitlyn Darnell, priest in the diocese of Upper South Carolina, co-editor of arts and culture for *Earth and Altar Magazine*, earthandaltarmag.org

If you are looking for a "quick fix" guide to the magical relationship, this is not your book. What you will read here is far more compelling, far more deep, and most importantly, far more real. Couples therapy experts Dr. Merck and Dr. Montanez deliver a beautiful and whimsical book in the form of a guide—an experiential exercise of loving, a love letter to the reader, to the work that has sustained them as clinicians, and to lovers who are interested in meaningful, textured relationships in a messy world. This book is a must-read for anyone who is interested in deepening their understanding of relationships, but perhaps most importantly, for those who have tried everything else and are giving it "one last chance." That, itself, speaks to the power of what Merck and Montanez have created for us all.

—Lara Sheehi, Assistant Professor of Clinical Psychology, The George Washington University

WISDOM FOR NAVIGATING YOUR
MESSY MARVELOUS LIFE

Love

A Guide to Life Partnering

AMY SANDER MONTANEZ

RHEA ANN MERCK

Managing Editor
Robbin Brent

Cover and Interior Design
Andrew Breitenberg

Compositor
Rick Soldin

Readers and General Suggestions
Caitlyn Darnell, Scott Gould, Mark Leviton,
April Pertuis, Kevin Roberts, Lara Sheehi

Messy Marvelous Logo Design
Helen Johnson Creatives

Administrative Assistant and Manager of Everything
Karen Garrison

ISBN Printed edition: 978-1-7357870-2-2
ISBN Digital edition: 978-1-7357870-3-9

Printed in the United States of America

To all who are brave enough to invest in the healing power of a loving relationship.

May this book be a guide as you navigate the Messy Marvelous world of life partnering.

We believe in you.

Contents

Stage Four: Unexpected Setbacks

Stage Five: Decor

Acknowledgments

It is hard to describe the privilege of sitting with couples in the messes of their lives. When a couple comes to therapy and lays the raw reality of their shared world at our feet with a plea for help, we know we are holding a sacred entity, a fragile relationship in need of care, repair, healing, and hope. Each of us has worked with couples for over thirty years, and there are no words for the gratitude we feel for each and every one of these brave souls. The amount of honest reflection, willing hearts, and hard work done in our offices reflects the importance of these primary relationships. So to each and all of the couples who have trusted us and taught us how to be better therapists, this book is for you.

Once again, our talented editor, Robbin Brent, has encouraged, inspired, and challenged us to be the best writers we can be. She continues to believe in what we have to offer to the world and she gives us nothing but her best. Robbin, you are a genius at what you do, and we count ourselves blessed by working with you.

To those of you who have been following MessyMarvelous for years, we are truly thankful. When you read our blogs, watch our videos, leave us comments on Facebook and Instagram, and send us messages of love and support, it matters. We continue to work to reach out to the world and spread the news that life is messy, and that there are actionable skills that can help life be more marvelous.

There is a saying, *A therapist who has not done their own therapy is a fraud.* Just so you know we are not frauds. We have both been in couple's therapy and individual therapy.

from *Amy*

My husband Nick and I first hit the couple's therapy couch soon after our daughter Maria was born and Nick's mother died, which happened nearly simultaneously. We were such a mess that we are written up in Dr. Russell Haber's book, *Please Help Me with This Family*. Our names are disguised, thank God, because Russell chose to feature us as a whole chapter in his book! We have returned for therapy several times during the course of our life together. Now married 42 years, we are more in love than ever, and we thank God—literally—every day for our relationship. So here's to Nick, his devotion and loyalty, which continue to bless me and teach me how to do this thing we call marriage. I pray that our marriage can give hope to others.

from *Rhea*

I too have done a lot of my own therapeutic work—both as part of a couple and by myself. While the couples therapy did not end the way I wanted, the personal growth I experienced through the process of my divorce and after has brought me to my fullest and best self. Through a decade of dating in midlife, I have learned more about love, partnership, and myself than I ever expected and I am grateful to all of my teachers along the way. It was a long hard road. But this life I am co-creating with my new partner has made the messy struggle marvelous now. Thank you for that, sweet Alberto.

It is in the shelter of each other that people live.

—Irish Proverb

Introduction

Any sustained, loving relationship is a creative process, an art as we often tell our clients. When you enter into and then continue a love relationship, there are marvelous moments that bring two people together, flow smoothly, and build beautiful memories. There are also messy times—days, weeks, even sometimes messy years—when it takes considerable effort, energy, and patience to continue the relationship. This book offers twenty skills that may help you not only prevent, but perhaps even thrive through, those messy times.

When we were well into the writing of this book and at the stage of putting a little more "shape" to it, the metaphor of building a house seemed an apt one for relationship building. Why? Because our intimate relationships are the space in which we live.

Our homes are important to both of us. Between us, we have collective experience building a house, working on and living through major renovations of two of those, and purchasing six homes. We also enjoy looking at houses, touring houses, and dreaming about houses. We are passionate about our homes, and we are passionate about healthy relationships. The building or renovating of both require similar steps.

With that in mind, we have divided our relationship skills into building stages. But, as with all of life, relationships are rarely linear and you may find yourself bouncing from one stage to the next and back again. No worries. This is just a guide; use it as creatively as you like. These skills will equip you with tools for any stage of a love relationship. If your partnership does not work out, you have learned skills that will be helpful when you begin another one. If the relationship evolves into a long-term committed relationship, this guide is a resource to keep your skills honed and your messy more marvelous. You can't lose.

Stage One of building a healthy, loving relationship is the drawing of blueprints. This is the time to dream big and allow your visions to unfold. What would each of you like this relationship to look like and feel like? What are the must-haves? What are the absolutely nots? This is the time to envision together the possibilities for your loving journey. It's a time when a good amount of wisdom is needed. Your heart may be in the clouds, but your feet need to be on the ground, at least some of the time, if you are planning on moving forward in the journey. In this stage you may alternate between dreams and visions and extreme practicality. It is the stage where you may be aware of feeling happier and more at home than you have ever felt with anyone. It is also the stage where you both have to ask yourself two important questions: "Can we be our best selves with this person?" and, "Do we trust each other?"

Stage Two of building your relationship house is pouring a foundation. Whether you got here quickly or it took a little time, this stage is often an important period of transition in any relationship. Things are getting more real now. What are your boundaries with each other? Do you believe your partner is willing to be influenced by you and can respect the boundaries necessary for continuing the journey? Paying attention to the capacity the two of you have to successfully solve problems becomes more important at this stage, as does accepting this person for exactly who they are. If the plan is to go forward, your blueprints are going to take concrete shape now. You are excited as things unfold. Sometimes, this is a stage in which you double-check your huge decision. Are you sure you both are all in? Can you truly imagine a lifetime with this person, or is it time to wish them well and move on?

Stage Three: Framing, and Stage Four: Unexpected Setbacks are the more practical stages of building a relationship. You may be committed by this time—living together, engaged, or married.

Reality has clearly set in and you are now having to negotiate with each other's families. You are managing a budget together and you are learning how to keep your sex life alive and satisfying. When there are setbacks, which there surely will be, will this relationship move forward with hope and confidence or will it shrivel and die, poorly nourished through the hard times in life?

If you have made it to **Stage Five: Decor**, good for you. You are now making your relationship into a work of art by designing your couplehood into something that is uniquely yours. You will be enjoying the incredible fruits of your labor. Breathe it in, celebrate, and then be ready to revisit a previous stage, because that is how life and relationships work. We spiral up and down and back and forth in different stages of love and loving. If your relationship is alive and well, it will not be stagnant.

It has been said that any relationship needs to be renegotiated every seven years. We have another way of saying that. Every marriage has several marriages within it. As we stay open and honest with ourselves and with our partners, and as we unfold into new developmental stages of life, our wants and needs will likely change. Just like with a house, from time to time we will have maintenance, renovations, and new décor needs to navigate. We may have new and different boundaries. We may have to have more hard conversations. We may need more or less of something important.

from *Amy*

I would say that my husband and I are on our fourth marriage. The first one before children. The second one during the raising of our daughter. Next the empty nest and negotiating life without those responsibilities. And now, we are entering a whole new stage: wanting to work less hard, wanting more space for creativity, and wanting to savor every moment we have together. After years of marriage, I can honestly say every stage was MessyMarvelous and I wouldn't change a thing. I am where I am because of all we have been through together. I am glad we are on our fourth marriage.

from **Rhea**

Beginning at the young age of not quite 22, I spent 27 years married. I fully intended to be married to that person for my entire life but sometimes what we want just isn't in the cards. Consequently, I spent the next decade living single, dating (a lot—which was decidedly messy), teaching the Psychology of Marriage (a truly marvelous experience), and doing more training and practice than ever in couples counseling. Suffice it to say, I have examined marriage and intimate relationships from every angle possible. While I *might* have changed some things along this bumpy and yet scenic road, I have learned valuable lessons about myself and others. That solo decade challenged everything I thought I believed about love, relationships, and how to be successful in them. For that relationship wisdom, I am eternally grateful and have every confidence that my current partner and I will continue to benefit from these hard-won life lessons. I also believe I am now in a relationship that will take me to the end of my days. And I am grateful beyond measure.

Love is not just some external thing that comes and goes. Love is something that you show, that you act upon.
—Esther Perel, *Where Should We Begin?*

"Love makes the world go round," as the old saying goes. But many couples also get cooked in the cauldron of love. Why is this? Because love not only takes commitment, love also takes skills, specific behaviors that make love more possible. We think this is not talked about enough or taught enough. Love takes surrender, letting go of some things to have more meaningful things. Love takes sacrifice and compromise, being flexible about your wants and needs in exchange for something that might be bigger and better. Love takes self-knowledge, understanding who you are and what you bring or don't bring with you. And all of that together—the skillful weaving and knotting, the ripping out and adding back in, the dedication and commitment of self and time, and the thoughtful self-reflection—create what will hopefully be your unique and astonishing work of art we call love.

The research we tend to turn to in the field of marriage and relationships is that of Drs. John and Julie Gottman at the University of Washington in Seattle, and the founders of the Gottman Institute. We reference them often because their work has transformed our understanding in the field of couples' counseling. No matter what we read or listen to about the science of marriage and relationships in general, the Gottmans' work is noted. The name *Gottman* has become synonymous with marriage and effective relationships. We reference them individually, as a couple, the Institute and its associates, and their research interchangeably throughout the book.

Each of us has had the privilege of soaking up the wisdom of elders who are no longer with us. Carl Whitaker, MD, affectionately known as the grandfather of family therapy, and Virginia Satir, MSW, known as the mother of family therapy, understood the need for a systemic perspective of our intimate relationships. The father-son team of Drs. Tom and Pat Malone, psychiatrists, taught us about the power of intimacy and the need to focus on the unique experience of the couple.

We understand that many beautiful, loving relationships happen outside the bounds of marriage. For the purposes of this book, we use the terms marriage and partnership interchangeably.

As with our first book, *LAUNCH: A Guide to Adulting*, we have designed this book to be used by individuals, but it is also designed to be used with your partner. The questions and reflections following the introduction of each skill are there to help open the conversation and get your creative juices flowing. Our suggestions will get you started, but we encourage you to continue your own research and discovery. There are many resources available to help you to enrich and improve your relationship.

Good luck to you as you create or strengthen your life partnership. It will be messy and it will be marvelous.

Amy & Rhea

Every new home build or home renovation requires a good set of plans.

As you either begin—or deepen—a relationship that you hope will be a lasting one, pay attention to what you need and want.

What are your must haves? What are the deal breakers?

Each person contributes to the building of the relationship.

What do each of you bring to the design of this significant relationship?

When choosing a life partner, look as far into the future as you can and see what is required in the goal you have chosen to pursue and get someone who is as hungry and as interested in those goals as you.

—Magnus Nwagu Amudi

Choose Your Partner Carefully

by *Amy*

I believe the most important decision you will make in your life is whom to marry, or if you choose, whom to make your life partner. This decision will affect your day-to-day life more than anything else. It is more important than where you go to college, what kind of job you have, how successful you are, or even how much money you make or earn. Life is messy, and having the right partner really does matter. If marriage—or a life-time partnership is part of your plan, I encourage you to choose carefully.

But how do you know? Can you be sure? Nothing is certain and marriage is at some point a giant leap of faith, but there are qualities and themes to which you might want to give your attention. I write from a place of a 42-year marriage, a professional practice where I have worked with hundreds of couples, and many friends and family with long-term marriages under their collective belts. Here's what I think.

Listen and watch carefully:
Your partner will tell you who they are.

When you are dating, you will hear things and learn things about your new favorite person. Pay attention. When you are in the throes of lust and the magical newness of a relationship, it is easy to overlook important cues. It is especially easy if you feel lonely or afraid that you will never meet the right person. Listen to what a person tells you. Be curious and ask many questions. Watch a person's actions, and question them if need be. As my doctor, John Gould, said to me about sickness—*If I listen carefully enough, the patient will tell me what is wrong*—the same is true in relationships. People will tell you and show you who they are.

I am reminded of a friend whose marriage ended after just a few years. She said recently that she missed the red flags that were waving mightily. He would routinely be late and would not call or text. This left her constantly accommodating his schedule. In the end she realized this was not just about his tardiness. It was about a complete lack of respect for her time—for her. Lack of respect will not bode well in a marriage. When someone has a good job but has no money saved, pay attention. Financial issues are problems in so many marriages. If your favorite person doesn't like your friends or is disrespectful to your family, open your eyes. A long-term relationship will break under that attitude. If a partner drinks too much, uses substances too much, loses their temper too often, pay attention. If your gut is telling you something is wrong, it just might be. Listen. Listen. Listen. Watch. Watch. Watch.

I encourage you to **be mindful of the person's character.** Are they honest and ethical humans? Are they willing to be transparent—about money, health issues, family issues—you know, the big things? Do they have your back, and you have no doubt that they are on your side? These questions are simple to write but require clear vision to discern. **Don't rush things.** And don't allow yourself to be rushed by the other person. Allow ample time to wipe the eyes of lust and love clear enough to see a person's true colors.

Make sure the big things are a match. If you are choosing a partner, perhaps for the first time, it is hard to imagine spending a lifetime with someone. It is hard to even imagine a lifetime. Hopefully, it is a long,

long time. And a lot will happen during that time. There will be lots of holidays, illnesses, deaths, moves, job changes, maybe children, political issues, financial issues, and perhaps tragedies. Life happens, over and over again, and you are going to be navigating this life with that person.

So what are the big things?

Family. What is this person's belief about what family means? How will you relate to each other's extended family? How will you balance the needs of extended family with your own nuclear family? Would you help support a family member financially? Would you ever allow a family member to live with you? How much of every holiday should be devoted to extended family. Work with your partner's family *(Skill No. 9)*.

I have shared a story from my early marriage with many couples. At the time it was a shocking moment for me. Now I see it as one of the wisest and most loving things my mother could have done for me. It was our first Christmas as a married couple. Nick and I thought very carefully about how we wanted to have our holiday unfold, and we decided that we would each go to our respective family homes for Christmas, me to New York and Nick to Florida, and then come back together for New Year's Eve. I called home to give my mom the good news. My mother's response was not what I expected. "Amy Jane (Ugh … using my middle name; I knew whatever was coming was serious.), you can come here with Nick, or you can go to Florida with him. You are married now, and you have to work these things out."

My mother's wisdom, which at the time felt like punishment, was a lesson in the necessity of negotiating important family issues and setting boundaries with our new families.

Children. Is this a marriage that will welcome children? If so, how many? How will child-care needs be distributed? Is adoption an option if infertility is an issue? Is there ever a time you would choose abortion? If this is a second marriage, how will step-children be welcomed and integrated? Do not treat these issues lightly. And don't make the mistake of assuming that a clearly stated preference will change over time. These issues matter deeply and can really wreak havoc if a couple is not on the same page.

Religion and Politics. While there are many "mixed marriages" that are happy and healthy, being aligned with each other's basic beliefs is important and can determine the amount of connectedness and unity a couple feels. At the very least, a deep respect and curiosity about each other's religious practices and political beliefs is important.

My husband and I occasionally speak to Rhea's Psychology of Marriage class at the local university. We talk a little about our marriage but mostly we answer student's questions. Every time we speak, one of the questions is: *"To what do you attribute the success of your marriage?"* Nick and I both have the same first answer—our personal and collective spiritual journeys. We both are committed to a faithful, Christ-led journey. More than that, though, we respect and are curious about each other's spiritual life. Where do you see God working in your life? How can I pray for you? We talk about our faith and attend church and conferences together *(Skill No. 19: Support and Encourage Each Other's Spiritual Journey)*. The question the students ask has more complex answers, but this has always been our first response.

Money. I don't know a couple who hasn't had at least one major fight over money. Money is one of the most emotional topics in marriages, and couples who have a shared attitude about money will have conquered one of the most sensitive issues of a marriage. Money means so many different things to people. It can represent safety, security, power, control, autonomy, pride, possessions, and freedom. It is also, like sex, one of the topics couples least like to talk about.

When you are deciding on a life partner, have the hard conversations *(Skill No. 13)* about money. What does money mean? What is yours? Mine? How do we combine our money? What does transparency about money mean? Accountability? Can we see each other's accounts? How much do we save? Give away? What would feel like financial infidelity? Do it *(Skill No. 12)*. Get on the same spreadsheet *(Skill No. 10)*.

Other Important Things

Compatible and Complementary. A balance of having similarities and differences can keep things alive and juicy. Maybe you are better with money and she is better at cooking. Perhaps he likes to do laundry and you like to do yard work. A separation of tasks can be very helpful. It is also important, though, to be compatible. Do you have ways of recreating together? Do you both like to travel? Are you foodies who love to explore new recipes and restaurants together? Is there volunteer work that matters to both of you? Are health and fitness important? These are things that bring a couple together and help create a sense of connection.

Sexual Attraction and Compatibility. Yes, this matters. A good sex life can be like glue in a relationship. It should be fun and fulfilling. It is also a reminder of who you are as a couple. But don't be fooled by the beginning stages of lust and romance in a dating relationship. This will eventually wear off, or settle down at least, and then you are left with your general attraction to your partner.

Love is not enough. I have said this often and it seems to shock people. But I believe it so deeply that it bears repeating here. **You have to like and respect your chosen partner.** This is different from loving them. Liking someone,—enjoying their company, wanting to be with them, respecting how they move through the world—these are the things that will carry you through in the end. Do you admire their virtues?

Are they kind, generous, thoughtful, tender, hard-working, honest, empathic, reliable, helpful? Are they willing to dig deep, do the hard work, accept responsibility for their behavior?

Pick well, Friends. Life is messy enough. Having a good partner matters. And don't worry, in the next chapter we will be talking about being a good partner. It's a two-way connection, for sure.

LOVE Questions for Reflection and Discussion

Even though The Beatles sing, "All you need is love," we wrote, "Love is not enough." What do you think about this?

What are the primary values that you and your partner share?

How would you know if you were giving up too much of yourself in a relationship? Are there topics you hesitate to bring up because you think it will cause problems?

What do your trusted friends and family think of your chosen love? Can you hear their concerns?

LOVE Checklist

- ☐ Do a value's clarification together. You can find one on messymar velous.com/tag/values-clarification/. Make sure your values are compatible.

- ☐ Make a list of the things you like and the things you don't like about your partner. Be honest.

- ☐ Poll your most trusted friends. Ask for their honest feedback. What do they see as your strengths and potential worries as a couple?

- ☐ As a couple, talk to older couples. Ask them their best advice about choosing a partner and about marriage.

- ☐ Have the hard conversations about the money, children, values, sex—all the things!

LOVE Resources

- Card Deck: *52 Questions before Moving in or Marriage.* gottman .com/product/52-questions-marriage-moving-card-deck/. This fun card deck asks wonderful conversation starters for couples ready to enter a deeper commitment. It can be purchased from their online store.

- *Eight Dates*, by John Gottman

- Apps: Gottman Card Decks: Including Date Questions, Rituals of Connection, Expressing Needs, and Empathy.

Notes:

The goal is not to be better than the other man, but your previous self.

—The Dalai Lama

Be Your Best Self

by *Rhea*

You've heard the question, "Is he/she THE one?" Equally important is the question, "Are YOU the ONE?"

I have a confession to make: I am not a fan of sweatpants. Of course, I don't want to offend anyone who loves them; they're just not my thing. And I don't judge you. I have plenty of clothing items that are equivalents, if not worse—baggy, comfy, and DEFinitely NOT flattering. When I whipped out a hoodie one cold night, I shocked one of my friends, who said, "I didn't even know you owned a hoodie!" *Of course I do.*

Jerry Seinfeld once said to his sidekick, George, "You know the message you're sending out to the world with these sweatpants? You're telling the world, 'I give up. I can't compete in normal society. I'm miserable, so I might as well be comfortable'" (Season 4, *The Pilot*). Over 20 years later, Eva Mendes made the mistake of saying, "Ladies, the number one cause of divorce in America is sweatpants." Her boyfriend, Ryan Gosling, had to come to her defense with his own admission of wearing sweatpants because people attacked her so harshly.

Obviously, this is not about sweatpants. It's not even entirely about how you dress. It *IS* about how you present yourself and what you communicate to your partner with your presence. It *IS* about what you are prepared to give and how you show up for your partner. Like George Costanza, do you communicate "I've given up" or, instead, "I am showing up as my best self"?

Maybe we are relationally lazy. Before you take offense or get defensive, let me ask: Have you ever wondered if the things you've done to get a relationship started, you later allowed to slip away? Why do we ever believe it's okay to present our best self to the world and then offer our partners the very worst version of ourselves? Maybe we are hardwired for complacency or, more positively spun, maybe we seek efficiency—which, of course, is like an "energy-saving" switch.

Let me give you some examples of people who have let their relationships slip and have quit bringing their best self.

- A couple is dating three years and she confides: "We haven't had sex in three months."

- A couple who are married 15 years: "I can't remember the last time the two of us spent an evening alone."

- A woman married 25 years: "Why should I care what I wear out? He's seen me at my worst."

- A man married 35 years: "I'm tired of talking about things with her—what's the point? I know what she thinks."

- Anyone: "Our relationship is set—we don't have to do all that (*fill in the blank*) we did when we were (*young/not married/first met*)." But is it?

When I read between the lines of these comments, this is what I hear: "I just don't think I care that much anymore." … "It's not worth my energy." Is that the best we can do? Is that how we show up for our partner? It's kind of a sweatpants attitude: *I've given up.*

Why do we give up so easily?

1. Because **we are busy**. Ask anyone around you how they're doing and chances are, they'll respond with some form of "busy." It has become so commonplace and stale, I am challenging myself to say ANYTHING but that (yawn)! But the fact remains, *yes*, we are all busy *and* we make choices about where we invest our time, energy, and resources. Is your relationship a priority in spite of your busyness?

2. Because **we take for granted** that what we have will always be there. Our cultural plot is that we no longer have to try once we've found a partner—we've trapped our 'catch.' End of story, right? Now that we've locked in on our partner and have some commitment and security, we don't have to worry that anything will disrupt our connection, right? *Wrong.* ... Sorry to say but anything left unattended can die. Although declining in recent years, the divorce rate still hovers in the 50% range.

3. Because **"for better or for worse."** This commitment, common in marriage vows, has become a misleading expectation. I feel pretty confident that the intended meaning involves issues like losing a job, financial hardship, being diagnosed with a chronic illness, dealing with a troubled child, or other family challenges.

   It does NOT mean that I don't care what you think; I don't take care of myself; I show up at home with nothing left for the life of the partnership or family; I treat everyone at home terribly because I personally feel terrible for whatever reason.

Look—we all mess up. We say things we don't mean (and hopefully learn from that awful experience). We don't always have the energy to be our best, but we owe it to our own sense of self-worth and the value we place on our relationships to do better. And to apologize when we mess up *(Skill No. 17)*.

Do the best you can until you know better.
Then when you know better, do better.
— Maya Angelou

What inspires us in our own lives makes us attractive to others. This rule of attraction applies whether you are on the market or not. My own partner refers to this as admiration. He wisely believes that admiration is a key component to long-term relationships and marriage. Social beauty standards can be short-lived as we age, and we will need more than that to remain attractive to our partner.

So how do we do this? **How do we become our best selves?**

1. **Take a long look in the mirror** (Literally and metaphorically). Do YOU want to hang out with YOU? Are you living as your best self? Are you putting your best self forward? What makes you interesting? Why have you given up on those things you *say* are so important to you? If you have not been tending to your health—physical or mental—what's that about? If you quit caring about you, what are you communicating to your partner and to the world? If you are suffering with mental illness, you need to know that these conditions are treatable and you should not resign yourself to a life in which this becomes an identity rather than a manageable challenge.

2. **Know yourself.** Do you truly know yourself? What are you passionate about? How do you spend your time, energy, and resources? What are your strengths? What are you like at your worst? Energy invested in your own personal and spiritual growth and development pays off.

3. **Dive deeper.** What do you bring to a relationship? Despite my diatribe on sweatpants, this is about much more than appearance.

Remember that a beautifully wrapped present doesn't mean much if the box is empty. Six packs, flawless skin, and the latest fashion eventually wear thin in a relationship. Ever sit with someone who can only talk about their work-outs or shopping (yawn)? I have (yawn again). Dig a little deeper into your core self—how do you want people to know you in this world? In what areas could you improve?

4. **Practice resilience.** How do you handle hardship? Many people sink easily into the comfortable cushion of complaining and playing the victim of their circumstances because it takes little effort to adopt this position. Others see hardship as a challenge. The fact is that we will ALL face messy situations throughout our lives—that's exactly how MessyMarvelous began! Some of the characteristics of resilient people include self-awareness, empathy, motivation, curiosity, and flexibility. Resilient people are realistic, keep good boundaries, trust themselves, manage emotions, and remain calm in stressful situations.

5. **Work on finding your life's purpose and meaning.** Dr. Martin Seligman has been researching positive psychology and happiness since the 1980s and has found that three types of lifestyles contribute to a happy life: a pleasant life, an engaged life, and a meaningful life. Finding joy happens more often when you are engaged and finding meaning and purpose in your life. We tend to want to seek out the pleasant life (having fun and creating enjoyment in our activities), but this actually contributes less to overall happiness than the other two. Why are you on this planet? What captivates you in such a way that you lose track of time? Are there things in life that connect you to something greater than just yourself?

Amy and I have a friend who embodies these principles. Gordon used to work in a field involving extracurricular activities and leadership training with college students. It was fun, fun, fun. He was well-liked, good at his job, and he enjoyed it. Until he didn't. It was much like that beautifully wrapped, empty box, and he found himself in a bit of a midlife awakening: "I needed to do something with more purpose. Something with more meaning in the bigger scheme of this world." He looked a long time, considered many options, and did a deep dive into his belief system and values. Eventually, Gordon found a place working to get fresh produce to low-income folks in food deserts. In addition to low-cost fresh foods, the not-for-profit provides recipes to help people develop comfort and familiarity with fresh foods, much the same way that boxed foods come with directions. It combined his interests in health and wellness, mission work, and cooking. Gordon is now fully living as his best self and bringing that best self home with him.

So think about it. Are you a sweatpants person? Have you given up? What are the messages you send your partner with your allotment of time, attention, curiosity, and your Self? When you put your best self fully into your life, it will spread out into your relationship, and I bet your partner will notice. I would also bet a lot of other people will notice and want to spend their time, energy, and resources with you.

No matter who you are, no matter what you did, no matter where you've come from, you can always change, become a better version of yourself.
—Madonna

LOVE Questions for Reflection and Discussion

What are some of the ways you have gotten lazy about yourself?

How do you stay accountable around investing energy into being your best self? Are there others who can help hold you accountable for being your best self?

What do you think of the saying, "Your partner should always accept you at your worst"? Do you think of this as a positive statement, or as an excuse to not put the effort into being your best self?

If nobody is looking, do you still do the basics, taking care of your physical, mental, and spiritual well-being?

LOVE Checklist

☐ Make a self-improvement checklist. Where in your life do you know you need to be better or do better? Start with one area. Master that before you move on to the next.

☐ Choose a mentor. With this person seek out hard truths about ways you could be a better partner. Pick someone who knows you, will be honest with you, and wants the best for you.

☐ Practice humility. Learn to apologize *(Skill No. 17)*.

☐ Spend more time in meditation and prayer. When the mind is quieted and still, much can be revealed and often the answers and healing we seek are found in the silence.

☐ If you are struggling with anything that brings up feelings of shame or trauma, get help *(Skill No. 14: Ask for Help)*. This is especially true if there has been unrevealed sexual abuse, addictions of any kind, or any other secretive issue that is creating a personal or interpersonal problem for you.

☐ Grab your journal and answer the questions under *How do we become our best selves?* on pp 34–35.

LOVE Resources

Find a good therapist. Seriously, in many ways there is no substitute for engaging in therapy as a way of being your best self. The website psychologytoday.com can help you find a therapist in your area with credentials to meet your needs.

The New Era of Positive Psychology TED Talk, Martin Seligman

Flourish, by Martin Seligman

- *The Wisdom of the Enneagram,* by Don Richard Riso and Russ Hudson

- *StrengthsFinders 2.0,* by Tom Rath

- Resilience Resources: apa.org/topics/resilience/

In real love you want the other person's good. In romantic love, you want the other person.

—Margaret Anderson

Check Your Romantic Fantasies

by *Amy*

Are you still aglow from last night's date during which you got lost in each other's eyes, finished each other's sentences, and couldn't sleep for all of the dreams and fantasies running amok? Or maybe you're still looking for your unicorn? Either way, romance is marvelous, and when reality sets in, terribly messy.

We all know "romance" is a favorite genre of literature. But according to Merriam-Webster, romance is also "something (as an extravagant story or account) that lacks basis in fact." Or the verb *romance*, "to talk about something in a way that makes it seem better than it really is." As in romantic fantasy—*not* romantic reality.

I don't know anyone who doesn't want at least some romance in a love relationship. This can be as simple as a loving text message or an extra-long hug or kiss before leaving for the day. It may look like evenings at home together with a pizza and a glass of wine, or an original poem or song written just for you. Or it may be more extravagant, like a surprise trip out of town to a memorable spot. Romance comes in forms as unique as people themselves.

The problem with romance is not the romance itself. It's when we start to believe the fantasy and lose track of reality. When we idealize anything, but especially a partner, we are setting ourselves up for a rupture of that idealization. One of my mentors, Carl Whitaker, put it this way: "If you put your partner up on a pedestal, all you will get is a stiff neck!" A metaphorical ruptured cervical disc is sure to be on the way if you don't have yourself firmly grounded in reality. And this takes time.

The curse of the romantic is a greed for dreams, an intensity of expectation, that, in the end, diminishes the reality. —Marya Mannes

It is only in the last half-century that marriages have been loaded with expectations too large to bear. We are supposed to be each other's best friend, sexual soulmate, travel companion, financial foundation, and prayer partner, as well as their sense of belonging, identity, and familiarity. And for all our adult lives, we are to continue to give each other a thrill, while we live longer than ever before. It is too, too much.

I want to tell you an embarrassing story about my own romantic fantasies gone awry. Occasionally there would be a Friday when I knew I would get off early. My husband **was supposed** to (but almost never did) get off at 1pm on Fridays. So, I would get this whole idea in my head, (note previous definitions) and it went something like this. "Oh, so Nick and I will go to some restaurant and sit outside and have a drink or two. Then we will go home and make love. Then we will go out for a lovely dinner and enjoy my favorite bottle of wine." **Please note:** I NEVER told Nick about my romantic fantasy. So, when Nick would call around 2pm and say he was stuck out of town and wouldn't be home until 7pm, which if I had been seeing things clearly I would have expected, I would ... well, I will let you imagine what I would do. It wasn't pretty. You see, my romantic fantasy was a secret that had no basis in fact (see previous definition, again). It took me a few years of marriage and a few thousand dollars of therapy to get it into my thick head that I was actually setting up a romantic failure. Now, I at least tell Nick about my fantasies. And I accept the realities of his job and of who he is much more fully. Now our romance is rooted in reality. It is sooo much better.

When I work with anyone in my office in the throes of a new romance, I always tell them to enjoy it. Have fun. Soak it in. And remember, it is not real yet. It takes a while for the trance to be broken and for the reality of another—a real human being—to show up. In my experience it takes at least a year, sometimes more. You have to get through holidays, flu season, tax season, travels, anniversaries, family vacations, and other big events to really get a feel for someone. You see, in the beginning, we think the other person will always be who we expect them to be, forever. And this feeling, this thought, soothes us and makes us feel safe.

And at some point, after a rupture, the real relationship begins, and we see the other person as an individual, with their own history, their own issues, their own strengths and weaknesses. Life happens, and this person may or may not react as we wish they would. We have to wrestle with who they are and who we are. The romantic dependence now has the opportunity to evolve into a mature interdependence. And that, Friends, is hard work. It is the work of a lifetime.

Sometimes the rupture happens when our romantic partner behaves in a way that shocks us. We have choices at this point. We can rationalize the behavior, we can address the behavior and test the solidity of our connection, or we can leave. If we think we cannot live without this person, we will probably minimize the behavior. We might also try to manipulate the person to keep them from repeating the same behavior.

This will never work long term, of course, and if it does, we will pay a hefty price. If we are with another human who is interested in an evolving, growing, transformational relationship, a relationship of resonance and support, we can probably work through things. If we are too shocked or horrified, or see this as a foretaste of things to come, we can leave.

Closeness and Intimacy

I have studied many good models of love in my life. The late Drs. Tom and Pat Malone, a father-son team and authors of *The Art Of Intimacy*, taught that love was based on closeness and intimacy. Closeness is like the family business; we zig and zag well, the bills get paid, we get the kids to school on time, and we can manage our lives. Intimacy is the capacity to show up with all of who I am while you show up with all of who you are (another word for this is sovereignty), and then we work at connecting and supporting each other. Closeness is safe and can also be dry. Intimacy is chaotic and also juicy. We need both.

Connection and Autonomy

I have also heard that love is made up of two pillars: Connection and Autonomy. The concept is very similar. For some, connection feels safe and autonomy feels risky. For others, connection can feel risky and autonomy feels safe. Either way, can the relationship tolerate both? This is at least a peek at what love can look like. When the fantasy is in check and the reality is in plain sight, can we hold the necessary paradox that will help a relationship thrive?

A friend of mine at church looked uncharacteristically grim one morning as I greeted him at the coffee pot before Sunday School. "How are you doing today?" I asked. He said, "You know, when I said *for better or for worse at* the altar, I thought it meant that when my wife was a little bitchy I would have to put up with it and find a way to help her. I didn't think it was going to mean having my father-in-law move into my house after a hip replacement while my wife is suffering from an autoimmune issue. You know? I just didn't think that's what it would be." Yeah. Any relationship fantasy is surely ruptured after a reality like that. But these are the unknowns when you marry. None of us know what life, or fate, will bring to us. Are we capable of closeness AND intimacy, of connection AND autonomy? Can we show up with our sovereign selves and find a way forward together that is respectful and supportive?

In order for love relationships to move beyond a state of trance and dependency, we need to check those romantic fantasies. Enjoy them, each and every one, AND have them balanced with the reality of your partner and your life.

Relationships are messy enough without the continued disappointments of a failed romance. Keep your expectations in check, and enjoy what can surely be marvelous.

LOVE Questions for Reflection and Discussion

How comfortable are you sharing your romantic hopes and wishes? What do you think about the saying, "If I have to tell him/her what I want, then it doesn't count"?

What does "for better or for worse" mean to you? What's the worst that you can imagine?

Which does your relationship do better with, closeness or intimacy? Connection or individuation?

How often are you willing to "play along" because your partner requests something you're not wild about?

LOVE Checklist

- [ ] Name three times when you have asked your partner for what you needed or wanted. If you can't, practice one this week.

- [ ] Take turns doing the emotional labor required for romance. Alternate who plans the dates and takes care of the details (childcare, tickets, reservations, etc.).

- [ ] Have scheduled meetings when you can talk about the closeness and intimacy of your relationship. What's working? What's not working?

LOVE Resources

- *Hold Me Tight,* by Sue Johnson

- *Where Should We Begin?* Podcast with Ester Perel

- *4 Habits of ALL Healthy Relationships,* TEDxSquareMile talk, Dr. Andrea and Jon Taylor-Cummings

Trust is the glue of life. It's the most essential ingredient in effective communication. It's the foundational principle that holds all relationships.

—Stephen R. Covey

Build Trust

by *Amy*

So you've found the right partner, you are the right partner, and your feet are firmly on the ground, at least some of the time. Time to consider a skill that makes or breaks a relationship.

It is universally believed that trust is non-negotiable for a long-lasting relationship. It is important in the beginning, middle, and on-going stages of any partnership. In these early stages, trust is built slowly as you get to know each other. But trust is one of those words that we all use but have difficulty defining.

So, how would you define trust? Do any of these questions sound familiar?

- 💜 Can I trust you to be there for me?
- 💜 Can I trust you to care for the children?
- 💜 Can I trust you to prioritize me over your mother/father?
- 💜 Can I trust you to regulate your intense emotions?
- 💜 Can I trust you to be transparent with me and not keep secrets?
- 💜 Can I trust you with money?
- 💜 Can I trust that you will treat me with respect and dignity?
- 💜 Can I trust you to work for our family's well-being?

♥ Can I trust that my well-being is as important to you as yours?

♥ Can I trust that you won't abuse drugs, alcohol, pornography?

Social scientists have determined that trustworthiness is the number one desirable trait in a partner. That does not come as a surprise to me but what does trust mean? What does it look like? How can we define this? And how can we build trust?

We are not noble by birth.
We are noble only by virtue of the way we think,
speak, and act. —Thich Nhat Hanh, *Fidelity: How to*
Create a Loving Relationship That Lasts

Preeminent couple's researchers, John and Julie Gottman, have studied this word—*trust*—for years. In research that spanned over twenty years, they found the word trust to mean that *in any interaction, a partner's behavior is acting in the best interest of both people.* This means even when we are having the hard conversations *(Skill No. 13)*, I believe my partner wants the relationship to come out on top. In other words, this is not an "I win-you lose" strategy. This is a win/win state of mind.

Do you have your own definition of trust? Here's mine: **Trust is a state of being that exists between two or more people who believe that they are safe and protected in a relationship.** And this state of being does not just exist in the big parts of our relationships, like fidelity. Trust is often developed in the small moments of our lives together. When I say I will be home at a certain time, am I? And if I am not, do I call? When I say I will take responsibility for a certain chore in our household, will I do that without being reminded? When I mess up, will I take personal responsibility for my behavior rather than deflecting blame or becoming defensive?

Trust is also built in moments when we connect emotionally with our partners. We must notice them, actually look at and talk with them during our day. When we do this regularly we will notice changes. Are there dark circles under the eyes? Is there a distance in their gaze? Are they avoiding eye contact? Do they seem "not like themselves"? Anything look different? Do we notice stress? Exhaustion? Happiness? And then we must want to ask. "Hey, you seem really tired. How are you?" Or, "What's up? You haven't been yourself lately. Is everything okay at work?" These moments of noticing and caring are the small ways we build trust over time.

Science tells us that when we have conversations like these, our bodies actually secrete oxytocin, the bonding hormone. This is the same hormone that is secreted when a person has an orgasm, and the more intense the orgasm, the more oxytocin is released. So conversations, like orgasms, that connect us emotionally, builds a sense of bonding and trust.

Trust is like a mirror, you can fix it if it's broken, but you can still see the crack in that mother fucker's reflection. —Lady Gaga

A chapter on trust would not be complete without some discussion on infidelity. Perhaps perceived as the most egregious betrayal, sexual infidelity brings many couples to the therapy couch. It might be a full-on affair that has lasted for a while. It could be a one-night stand. An on-going secretive relationship with pornography might be considered a sexual betrayal. In any case, sexual infidelity is a common presentation in a therapist's office. And the question most often asked is: "How can I ever trust him/her again?"

One of my mentors in the field, the late Carl Whitaker, said this about trust: **"There is no such thing as trust. There is only the willingness**

to risk being hurt again." Please re-read that sentence. Again. What do you feel? When I heard Carl say these words in a live supervision session, I was a young 34-year-old therapist, and I was a little shocked. It took me a while to understand the significance of this statement. These words give the betrayed person autonomy and sovereignty. In other words, has enough emotional work been done? Do I understand myself more, do I have a strong enough belief that the other person will actually not do this thing to me again, that I am willing to take the risk? Because nothing is 100%. I often ask my clients, "IF this happens again, are you sure you will survive?" You have to know the answer to this question is a "Yes" in order to re-engage with the betraying partner. Dan Yashimoto, a student of the Gottmans', came up with the idea that the basis for building trust is the process of ATTUNEMENT in a couple's relationship. That process looks like this:

Awareness of your partner's emotion

Turning toward the emotion

Tolerance of two different viewpoints

Understanding your partner—or at least trying to

Non-defensive responses to your partner

Empathic responses to your partner

Every time we attune to our partners, we are building trust and empathy. It is the work of a lifetime. It is also easier the more we practice.

Trust is a foundational issue in any true partnership. We usually don't receive trust immediately nor give it immediately. It is built slowly, over time, as we learn to understand the other person and attune to them. It is increased when we realize that a good relationship is not a "win-lose" proposition, but is a "win-win" proposition.

Building trust can be messy and marvelous. One thing I know for sure; there is no successful way forward without it.

LOVE Questions for Reflection and Discussion

What does trust mean to you? Write your own definition.

How trustworthy are you on the little things? The daily moments? When you say you will do something, can you be counted on to follow through?

In your family of origin, who were the people who were trustworthy? How did you know this? Were there people who broke your trust? What was that like for you?

How has trust been managed in your previous relationships? Think in terms of yourself and your partner. What are the ways you have or have not yet healed from broken trust in a relationship? How do you allow resentments to shape you?

LOVE Checklist

☐ Take your definition of trust and then discuss it with your partner.

☐ How well do you believe you ATTUNE to your partner? Ask them how you are doing? Rank yourself on each of the six micro-skills necessary to ATTUNE. If it feels safe, ask your partner to do this for you, and do it for them.

☐ Practice a daily review. At the end of each day, look back honestly and name the moments in which you were or were not trustworthy. This is a good accountability practice for a period of time to assess yourself.

☐ If you find you are struggling with being trustworthy, especially in the small things, ask for help to determine why this is a chronic struggle for you.

LOVE Resources

- *What Makes Love Last: How to Build Trust and Avoid Betrayal,* by John Gottman and Nan Silver

- *Why Won't You Apologize?* by Harriet Lerner

- *How to Build Trust and Positive Energy in Your Relationship Podcast* Episode #74 in *Relationship Alive* on Spotify, John Gottman

- There are dozens of podcasts available to help with rebuilding trust in a relationship. Try googling "podcasts on rebuilding trust in relationships" and find one that speaks to your needs.

Just like a stable house must rest upon a firm foundation, your relationship will also be built upon a foundation.

Inspect it carefully.

Pay attention to all aspects of the foundation, and don't assume a problem will magically correct itself as the building takes shape.

A foundation that is off by just five degrees will change the way the entire house rests.

So too with a life partnership.

Your personal boundaries protect the inner core of your identity and the right to your choices.

—Gerard Manley Hopkins

Manage Your Boundaries

by *Amy*

Knowing, setting, and respecting personal boundaries is foundational to a successful relationship.

At this time in our culture, the word *boundaries* is a buzzword. It shows up on dozens of Instagram sites, google it and you will be inundated with possible resources, and whole books are being published about this single but not simple issue. The word might be heard sitting outside at coffee shops, coming from the table next to yours. Or maybe your table. I have many conversations in my office and my home involving the concept of boundaries. So yes, knowing, establishing, and managing boundaries is its own important skill—I might even call it an art.

But just what is a boundary? A boundary, quite simply, is a limit. This is where you end and where I begin. A boundary honors ourselves as separate individuals, unique in our feelings, thoughts, and wants. That sounds easy unless you don't know what you need and want, or you don't honor what you need and want, and then a boundary can become very ambiguous. Knowing how to communicate who you are and becoming comfortable doing that is the beginning of setting boundaries. Another way to say this is that **a boundary is an external manifestation of an internal knowing.**

What are the different kinds of boundaries? In terms of love relationships, it might help to think in terms of material boundaries, personal/physical boundaries, and cognitive/emotional/spiritual boundaries. Of course these can overlap, but for the sake of getting a basic understanding, let's focus on these three.

1. **Material boundaries** are about how we manage our personal belongings in love relationships. These types of boundaries are usually quite tangible, but people have very individual needs and wants and it is best not to assume! Remember, when we *assume* it makes an *ass* out of *u* and *me*! Boundaries in this area may have been learned in our families (my father never went in my mother's purse), they may be personal preference (I don't like others driving my car), or they may be created due to past relational history (my ex always went through my mail and would use information against me). However you get to know your boundaries, clear communication about them is necessary in a healthy relationship.

   How do we mix our money? If I loan you money, how will you pay me back? Is it a gift? Do you have the code to my phone? The password to my social media accounts? The key to my home? How often do I want you to call me or text me during the work day? If I have a door shut, do I expect you to knock before you come in? Do you open my mail? Go in my purse? Are you allowed to use my car? And do I expect you to fill it up with gas if you do? These things may sound trivial to some, but it is in honoring the seemingly little things that we build trust and get to know someone more deeply. Usually we get to know these boundaries as we get to know our partner better.

2. **Personal and physical boundaries** have to do with our bodies and our sense of ourselves in space. In a love relationship these boundaries often come into play in the sexual area of our lives.

How do I want to be touched? What does consent mean? What means yes and what means no? What kind of access to my body do you get? Is it okay to wake me up in the middle of the night to have sex? Is it okay if I am under the influence? Do I want you in the bathroom when I am using it? Because we often feel vulnerable in this area, it may be more difficult to have conversations about physical boundaries. And if we are a survivor of sexual or physical abuse and trauma, we may find ourselves triggered and unable to effectively have a voice about these issues. If this is you, please refer back to Skill No. 14 *(Ask for Help)*. It is important to get support, guidance, and healing in this area and to want some third-party help to navigate these waters.

Physical boundaries may also play out in how much touch and affection we want in day-to-day life. Do I like to be hugged when I come home from work? If I am busy working, is it okay for you to interrupt me for a kiss or touch? Do we have boundaries about how we touch, hug, or kiss someone else?

3. **Cognitive, emotional, and spiritual boundaries** are perhaps the least tangible and the most subtle, difficult, yet vital boundaries to understand, establish, and enforce. These are the boundaries that have to do with how you guard your thoughts, feelings, and spirit, and how others relate to those. I hope you know that you have permission to feel whatever you are feeling. You do not have to have justification, proof, or even an understanding of what you are feeling in order to feel it. And no one has the right to tell you that "you shouldn't feel that way." You feel what you feel. It doesn't even have to make sense at the time, but usually, with some reflection and some psychological and spiritual savvy, we can figure out what we are feeling and why. And it certainly does not have to make sense to your partner. Your partner's job is to be curious enough to try and understand your feelings, and

even if they cannot, learning to accept them is part of the job. So being allowed to feel what you feel without being shamed, ridiculed, embarrassed, or dismissed is a boundary.

Similar to feelings, you are entitled to your own thoughts and opinions. You have the right to have them without being steam-rolled or labeled. When a partner talks over you, talks too loudly, or belittles your ideas, that is a boundary violation. If a partner is not willing to be curious about why you think what you think, and cannot respect the conclusions you have come to, digging deep to set a limit is necessary. If a partner is dismissive of your yearning for spiritual well-being, find your voice and set a boundary.

 "No" is a complete sentence. —Anne Lamott

One of the most painful states of being in a relationship is when one feels dishonored, manipulated, and exploited. When a partner has clearly crossed a boundary and then blames you. When a partner has lied and makes you feel like you are imagining things. When you remember something and your partner questions your memory to the point of making you question your sanity. There is a technical word for this: gaslighting. Gaslighting is one of the most painful boundary violations. If you suspect you are being gaslighted, *please get help.* Or if you know you do this to another person, please get help.

So you see, this is a complex topic. Here are some starting places when beginning to work on this skill.

Recognize what you are feeling. It might be clear, or you might need to practice what I tell my clients is "the pause." It is okay for you to say, "I need a minute to think about this." If you have trouble labeling your feelings, use a feeling wheel (on page

71) to help you. Feelings can be very nuanced, and it is okay to use a tool to help you have clarity.

Communicate with your partner. Set aside an appropriate time to have the hard conversations. If you tend to be a pleaser or an empath, this will be harder for you. Be gentle with yourself and your partner. This is how we really get to know someone.

Know when to hold fast and when to be flexible. Being physically or emotionally abused usually requires a rigid boundary. Some people have a once-and-done policy about this (*Skill No. 1: Choose Your Partner Carefully*). And yes, generally this is a good rule. However, there are exceptions to this. Once I threw my wallet at my husband. I had a small medical procedure that left me more knocked out than I expected and unable to eat. When he got home from work, my blood sugar was so low I was in a very compromised state. He did or said something that upset me, and I threw my wallet at him. I had never before nor since thrown anything at anyone. If he had had a rigid boundary about this we would be divorced. He wisely remained flexible, understood how compromised I was, and got some food in me quickly.

Setting appropriate boundaries requires a good bit of maturity. It also just takes time and practice. Like all important skills, we must decide to practice what we say we value.

LOVE Questions for Reflection and Discussion

In your family of origin, how were you encouraged to express your needs and wants? If you were not encouraged to do this, what lessons did you learn about needs and wants?

Some people feel guilty or ashamed when they start setting boundaries with a partner or with their children. Is this you? Ask yourself what these feelings are about and why these feelings are being triggered.

Which of the types of boundaries are hardest for you to set? Material, personal/physical, or cognitive/emotional/spiritual? What are your thoughts about why this is hard for you?

LOVE Checklist

☐ Keep a boundaries journal. In this journal, write down specific actions you have taken to set a boundary with a partner. Also journal about your partner's response and your feelings connected to this situation.

☐ In this boundaries journal, work to categorize the areas in which you struggle with boundaries. Some groupings might be work, volunteer positions, parents, big decisions, financial decisions, sexual life, etc. Examine your motives for not keeping boundaries in each area. Search out any patterns.

☐ Get some support and accountability from a friend or a mentor. Setting boundaries can be difficult work, especially at the beginning, and having help doing this can be a key component to your success.

☐ Practice, practice, practice.

LOVE Resources

Boundaries: When to Say Yes, How to Say No, by Drs. Henry Cloud and John Townsend

Set Boundaries, Find Peace: A Guide to Reclaiming Yourself, by Nedra Glover Tawwab

The Dance of Anger: A Women's Guide to Changing the Patterns of Intimate Relationships, by Harriet Lerner

Free download *How to Set Limits*: https://educate.crisispreven tion.com/Refresh—HowToSetLimits.html

Intimacy requires a huge tolerance for differences.

—Harriet Lerner, Ph.D.

Life Partnering Skill No. 6

Accept Each Other

by *Rhea*

If you want to see an excellent example of crumbling boundaries and lack of acceptance, watch the after-dinner party fight scene in *The Break-Up* with Jennifer Anniston and Vince Vaughn (available on YouTube).

In this painful five-minute scene, we get an honest look into a relationship that is falling apart. She desperately wants him to be different, and he placates her with what she wants to hear in order to appear as someone he is not. The scene is also a good example of breaking *every single* Fair-Fighting Rule *(Skill No. 15: Learn to Fight)*. In the plot, she is an art dealer with refined tastes and he is an average guy who is a tour-guide bus driver. Despite the obvious mismatch, they decide to live together and the relationship begins to unravel as **the reality of who they are** emerges. Neither one can accept the other.

That's the trouble about marriage. Women always hope it's going to change the husband. Men always hope it won't change their wives—and both are disappointed! This quote is from the 1930s play, *Cynara*, by H.M. Harwood and R. Gore-Browne. After the honeymoon, as life settles into a routine and reality comes into focus, the cloud of what the characters wanted to see about their partner dissipates. This happens to us too.

This relationship story is a common cause for conflict; a partner feels unseen because the other wants them to do or be someone who they are not. For example, one partner complains that the other refuses to participate in something that they enjoy. The refusing partner says, "You know I hate gardening. I have NEVER liked working in the yard. You knew that when you married me!" The requesting partner invariably feels rejected and hurt. Or the reverse may be true. One partner engages in an activity that the other has no interest in. The uninterested partner says, "I don't understand why you spend so much time volunteering. You're gone too much. Don't you want to be here at home with me?" The interested partner responds perplexed, "But you know I've always participated in volunteer work. It was part of what I did that you were attracted to when we were dating." Here are some common examples.

- *Why does he have to go (hunting/golfing/to play poker/to sporting events) EVERY week?*

- *Why does she (take yoga/dance classes/go shopping with her mom/ play tennis) SO much?*

- *Why doesn't he shave? Why does she live in yoga pants?*

- *Why won't he rent a tux and go to this gala with me?*

- *Why won't she go camping and fishing with me?*

- *Why do you work all the time? Why don't you ever DO anything?*

- *WHO ARE YOU?*

If you see your relationship in this, it's not surprising. It's part of the language of navigating closeness and distance; connection and autonomy. It's the sound of struggling with acceptance in committed relationships.

Why are we like this?

Often it is the very things that attract us to someone that then become a problem. You fall in love with him because he is so spontaneous, fun, and laid back. Or you fall in love with her because she is stable, hard-working, and nice. In the beginning, it's easy to view your partner in this positive light. But what happens when the easygoing, surfer guy doesn't get a job? Now he is lazy, irresponsible, and self-centered. And when that driven, career-focused gal spends a lot of time working in the evening, suddenly she is a boring workaholic who is no fun. Invariably, couples will describe the same basic characteristics of their partner in a positive light early on, then more negatively down the road as reality sets in.

We've all been there on some level. So how do we end up in this place? And more importantly, what do we do about it?

When reality sets in and beyond, there is potential for great growth. It takes two open partners willing to navigate rough waters to discover a new land of love. A relationship can grow deeper and richer when it moves beyond the superficial game of making oneself appealing. The great question is, **"Can I accept my partner for who they really are?"** And equally important, **"Can I accept the choices I made?"** If we don't practice accepting each other, the rejection of each partner's true self will result in distance and the hurt between them will only worsen over time.

Part of accepting who your partner is as a person is the task of accepting your partner's feelings. In parenting, for example, there is a guideline to be consistent—but that is consistency in your behavioral approaches, family rules, and expectations; it is rare that two parents have exactly the same ideas and definitely not the same feelings about situations with their kids. Accepting one another's feelings is a part of the task of accepting who they are by understanding their story, what shaped their experience, and thus, their emotions. **Just listen and accept.**

In *The Break-Up*, the emotions are hot and loud. There is little understanding or acceptance being practiced. It appears as if they are fighting about dishes, lemons, the ballet, and videogames. But they're not. They are struggling with much more over-arching dilemmas—what I think of as more universal problems in the struggle for acceptance. These universal themes can be translated into intrapersonal and interpersonal ULTRA Skills.

The 8 ULTRAS: Universal Long-Term Relationship Acceptance Skills

1. Accept that your own fantasies are not reality.

2. Accept that you are different people with differing backgrounds.

3. Accept that you bring different gifts and talents to the relationship.

4. Accept your partner's feelings and their style of thinking.

5. Accept that you cannot change your partner.

6. Accept that truth and reality can look different depending upon perspective.

7. Accept that your paths will be altered by life over the long run.

8. Accept that people change their minds about things small and large—this includes you!

We all want to be seen, known, and accepted for how we feel and who we are in our relationships and beyond. Our partners want that same thing—to be seen and loved for who they are. To be accepted. So be true to yourself and practice the 8 ULTRAS.

LOVE Questions for Reflection and Discussion

What are the traits in your partner that are positive *and* negative? And what about in you?

What are the hardest things for you to accept in your partner? Given that you cannot change your partner, is this a deal breaker?

Is there a need for a hard conversation *(Skill No. 13)* about something that is difficult to accept?

How well do you accept yourself? This is really a key point because if you are having trouble accepting yourself, it will be impossible to accept anyone else.

Notice times you struggle to simply accept your partner's feelings about something that is different than how you might feel or react. What is making you uncomfortable about these moments? How can you practice accepting these differences?

LOVE Checklist

☐ Read over the list of the 8 ULTRAS. In a journal, address these one at a time, asking yourself honestly how well you do with each item.

☐ With your partner, have a discussion about each of the ULTRA items.

☐ Print out the Feeling Wheel on page 71, hang it in an obvious place, and use it with your partner when you bump into difficulties with each other.

LOVE Resources

- *The Seven Principles That Make a Marriage Work,* by John and Julie Gottman

- *The New Rules of Marriage,* by Terrance Real

- *I Hear You: The Surprisingly Simple Skill Behind Extraordinary Relationships,* by Michael S. Sorensen.

- *Where Should We Begin?* Podcast, Ester Perel

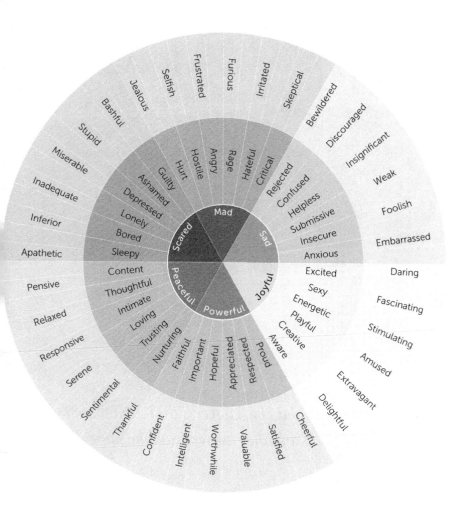

The Feeling Wheel
by Gloria Willcox

Gloria Willcox (1982) The Feeling Wheel, Transactional Analysis Journal, 12:4, 274-276,
vDOI: 10.1177/036215378201200411

Many marriages would be happier if the husband and wife clearly understood that they are really on the same side.

—Zig Ziglar

Accept Your Partner's Influence

by *Amy*

Good for you if you can accept your partner for who they are! Now, allowing your partner to influence your ideas, opinions, and choices is a skill for master relationship builders! Let me tell you a story.

Long ago, in the early months of our marriage, Saturday mornings were tense with disagreements about how we were going to spend our time. Were we going to work first (my German-Lutheran heritage), or were we going to play first (my husband's Latin, free-spirited background)? It was an early power struggle, and somehow, magic and grace I suspect, we figured out a compromise that involved rotating our process every other week. This week we play first, and then work. Next week we work first, and then play. On the weeks we played first, we didn't get as much work done. On the weeks we worked first, we didn't get in as much play. Neither one of us died. The house didn't fall apart and we didn't turn into irresponsible adults, either. Perhaps the compromise even changed us each a little. Maybe we learned that the other person's way had some merit to it. Yielding actually meant winning. It was a good lesson to begin learning as newlyweds, and young ones at that.

Forty-two years of marriage later, we have navigated many more power struggles. We have spent more than a few dollars on the marriage therapy couch. One of the biggest take-aways for me has been this: **If you want a vibrant, healthy, happy marriage, you need to accept each other's influence.**

What does that even mean? Accepting your partner's influence is primarily about two things: sharing power, and conveying honor and respect.

When I respectfully listen to my partner and believe that his or her opinion is as valuable as mine (one person, one vote as a friend of mine likes to say), I am capable of accepting influence. When I listen with the intention of learning more about what my partner is thinking and why, I am capable of accepting influence. When I can lay aside my own need to be right, I can begin to accept the influence of my partner.

Here's a story that is a compilation of situations I have encountered. These are not real people, but this is an accurate presentation.

Susie and Charlie have been married for 17 years. They are having great difficulty co-parenting their youngest child, who is quite persevering and willful. Susie reasons with her son, and although it is not particularly efficient, she usually gets the results she wants. Charlie takes a hard line and is often spanking and threatening his child. When he entered my office, he began the session by saying, "I don't even want to be here. I am not going to let anyone tell me how to raise my child. Including her." He points his finger at his wife. Susie is crying by now. This is the first five minutes. Charlie will not give his wife any credit for having some pertinent ideas as to what might work with their child. I stay away from the presenting problem, which of course isn't the problem at all. The problem is that Charlie will not accept the influence of his wife, his wife has become a nag and a vigilante, and their child is not receiving the benefit of an aligned parenting team. (And of course there are even deeper problems than that, which are important but not the topic of this chapter.)

Accepting influence can be easier if you break the problem into smaller pieces. For example, if you can't get totally on board with what your spouse is saying, can you find some part of what they are saying that you can understand? Some part that you could say, "Okay. I get that part." That shows a willingness to understand and can often ease tension.

Now I am going to say some politically incorrect things but please, do not stop reading. I have to say that the research shows that men have a more difficult time allowing their partners to influence them. And women tend to nag more and use harsher language. **It seems to be gender related.** Women ask for help and suggestions more naturally. Men more easily make decisions on their own. Women push early on for things to happen their way. Men allow for consequences to set in as a way of proving a point.

Are you still reading? Please keep reading. "Marriages where the husband resists sharing power are **four times more likely to end** or drone on unhappily than marriages where the husband does not resist" (Gottman, *The Seven Principles That Make a Marriage Work*). When a woman knows her partner will listen to and consider her influence, she is less likely be critical and harsh.

And if you are a man and you are reading this and you stop now, you are just proving the next politically incorrect, well-researched fact, which is that when men get defensive, shut down, stonewall, or escalate the aggressiveness of the conversation, they are just a breath away from a divorce. Oh, and even more politically incorrect but well-researched news, men who accept their wives influence are better fathers. Yup.

Women, you are not off the hook. Not even a little. Women, check your harsh language and your nagging criticism. It doesn't help. Ever. It will never win you his respect, his honor, or his admiration. Which is what you really want anyway, right? Unless what you really want is to be right. If that is the case, here's the question to ask yourself: Do you want to be right, or do you want to be in a relationship? Because sometimes you cannot have it both ways.

I once read an article titled, *She Divorced Me Because I Left Dishes by the Sink.* Authored by a man, it is a well-written example of what it means to accept influence. And why it is worth doing.

Before COVID-19 took over the planet, my husband and I enjoyed ballroom dancing. Dancing together in this way has been quite a lesson in accepting influence. We must work as a team. And even though in the ballroom the man "leads," it is always a team effort. Respecting each other's ways of doing things, being influenced by each other's rhythm, covering each other's mistakes, and being moved by each other's bodies are all necessary in the dance world. So the dance becomes a metaphor for life, for relationship, for commitment, and for trust.

Committed relationships are messy. They are challenging. The rewards for treating your partner with fondness, admiration, and genuine respect are too many to count. So accept your partner's influence, and you can look forward to a vibrant, happy, marvelous relationship.

LOVE Questions for Reflection and Discussion

In what areas are the biggest power struggles in your relationship? How do you accept your partner's influence in these areas?

How important is being right to you? Or doing things in a very specific way? What would help you be more flexible in these areas? Would you be willing to experiment?

Consider the times when you feel competitive rather than collaborative with your partner? Can you identify what triggers feelings of competition?

LOVE Checklist

☐ The next time you are caught in a push-pull competitive argument with your partner, try holding hands through your discussion.

☐ Find ways to move past the power struggle that is unique to your relationships. Some couples do better if they take a walk together. Others might be able to be less competitive if they are cooking together or traveling together.

☐ Make a list of what your partner is better at than you are. Can you allow them to lead in that area?

☐ Make a list of what punches your buttons. With your partner, discuss ways to handle that differently.

LOVE Resources

- *She Divorced Me Because I Left Dishes by the Sink,* by Matthew Fray, mustbethistalltoride.com

- *The Seven Principles That Make a Marriage Work,* by John and Julie Gottman

- *Husbands Can Only Be Influential If They Accept Influence,* by Jeff Pincus, gottman.com

Notes:

Every time you are tempted to react in the same old way, ask if you want to be a prisoner of the past or a pioneer of the future.

—Deepak Chopra

Be a Creative Problem Solver

by *Rhea*

"You can be right or you can be married." Ouch! We all like to be right, *right?* But at what cost? Creative problem solvers are able to move beyond the notion of right and wrong. And yet, some people are just *in it to win it.* If this dynamic is present in your relationship, accept the challenge to grow in this area.

I knew a very bright, successful couple who could not agree on a simple budget because managing money had become a power struggle. Who would win? His desire to save or her desire to have a stylish home? For them, the struggle was no longer about money, but rather, "Who will be in charge?"

Creative problem-solving begins with a decision tree. Is there a solution to this problem? Then SOLVE IT. While this sounds a bit simple, you'd be surprised how often couples do not do this. A couple with an income of over half a million dollars a year could not settle the problem of getting the grass cut. He agreed to do it and would then put it off. She was the one troubled by the look of the lawn. The co-therapist and I almost shouted at them in unison, "HIRE SOMEONE!" But clearly that was not the problem. The problem existed at a much deeper level—a rather unconscious one—about old scripts, trust (or the lack of it), and entitlement.

How to Be a Creative Problem Solver

There are several levels of creative problem-solving. Begin with the most simple and work your way down if the previous level did not work.

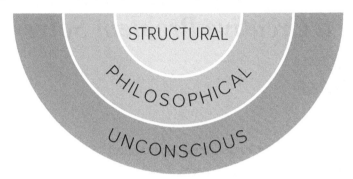

Structural Level. This is the "nuts and bolts" level of problem-solving. These are solutions that are practical and straightforward.

- 💜 We make a calendar for cooking dinner that takes into account the work week and each partner's obligations. Or we decide that one is much better at meal planning than the other and loves to cook so that person takes on the cooking and the other cleans up afterwards.

- 💜 Together a couple decides that one is more methodical and appreciates structured tasks like bill-paying and financial planning while the other has a more project-oriented approach to things and prefers to plan vacations or research types of plants for the garden.

- 💜 There is one mutually-dreaded task that the couple decides to take turns mucking through it and marks it on the calendar.

If simple and structural doesn't work, what is going wrong? Many couples come in to our offices and start a session like this: "We had the worst fight—and it was over something really ridiculous." They talk about not being able to agree on household duties and division of labor, how to spend or save their money, or whether or not kid #1 should play soccer or football or take ballet. Over the years, many people have said to us, "We are two smart, educated people; why do we keep having the same stupid fight over and over?" When that happens, dig a little deeper—go to the next level.

Philosophical Level. At this level you are considering values in your personal life and in your relationship. Having conversations as a couple to uncover each person's values and desires may be necessary. Gottman refers to this as dream detection and believes conflict is the result of a hidden personal longing. Uncovering these longings and dreams helps open the door to more creative possibilities and fosters a better understanding of your partner.

Take child-rearing as an example. Let's say we have a discussion about how we want our family life to look when we have children. We agree that we both want to be involved in ways that blur the lines of traditional "mother" and "father" roles. We are both interested in sharing engagement in all aspects of parenting—from nightly baths, painting fingernails, throwing a ball, and first haircuts, to handling discipline, meeting with teachers, and overseeing homework. I'm not suggesting these conversations will be conflict-free but if you have mutually desired principles upon which you make decisions, you can be more creative as problem solvers.

This kind of philosophical negotiation is not a one-and-done conversation. Goals and dreams need to be revised along the way. There will be changes as a relationship enters new developmental stages and as your needs change, both individually and collectively as a family.

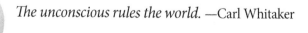

The unconscious rules the world. —Carl Whitaker

Unconscious Level. When you reach an impasse, as all couples do, considerably more reflection and negotiation is required. You will know you're there when you've dug in and are unwilling to negotiate. Gottman calls this gridlock. Oftentimes there are motivations that are not clearly in the awareness of either party. It takes some digging—deep, honest, personal reflection—to uncover why you are so stuck. This is also a good point at which to ask for help *(Skill No. 14)*: Call a therapist, seek counsel with your clergy, heck, or phone a true friend—someone who can be trusted to be honest with you about you. Your friend's role is not to critique your partner, but to ask questions to help you dig deeper. Some friends are not equipped to do that.

There are other reasons that people get stuck without understanding why they can't solve seemingly simple problems. Here are a few.

- **Poor communication and negotiation skills.** Many people fall short of creatively solving problems because they use a passive or passive-aggressive (or just straight up aggressive) style to attempt to communicate their needs and desires or to advocate for themselves. Practice assertive communication.

- **Old scripts.** These are the rules from our families of origin, our reflexive way of functioning. *We all have them.* Old scripts become **expectations**. Writer Anne Lamott said, "Expectations are resentments waiting to happen." This is a great time to put on your detective hat and discover your own internal stories. Then inquire with your partner about theirs.

- **Unmet needs.** So what are your deep desires? Your unspoken longings in the relationship? If you're not clear, it is doubtful your partner will know either *(Skill No. 3: Check Your Romantic Fantasies)*. Learn to know and ask for what you need.

🌱 **Fear.** We all have trepidations and fears that we may not give voice to—and even some about which we are unaware. Fear is not always rational or even reasonable but CAN be worked through when we bring it into the light. Just like in childhood, the fear of the monster in the closet rarely upsets us during the day or when we turn on the closet light and open the doors. Learn to say, "For whatever reason, I feel scared about this." Or, "I feel anxious about this decision." Or, "I need to figure out why I feel so bad about this."

🌱 **Trauma.** Trauma often resides in the unconscious. Our bodies and brains are designed to detect the most subtle similarities to past danger in an effort to keep us safe in the present. It happens in less than a millisecond and then our rational brain is totally offline for any creative problem-solving. Journaling, talking (with an experienced listener), and therapy can all help uncover these hidden and derailing experiences.

Get Creative. Virginia Satir said, "There are at least three possible solutions to every problem: your solution, my solution, and the ones we haven't thought of yet." In many spiritual traditions, this is also known as "the third way." These are the solutions we must seek, the ones that take us out of our "me vs. you" rut to the "we"—from competitive to collaborative. This requires empathy—the ability to examine a problem from another's perspective. To step outside of ourselves and be willing to take a risk.

How can we entertain options that go beyond one way of looking at things in order to embrace more creative solutions? A problem-solving strategy used by highly successful companies is brainstorming, particularly in groups. Brainstorming is the simple act of generating ideas, no matter how absurd or feasible. The purpose of brainstorming is to loosen up the system—to get the creative juices flowing. At its best, brainstorming could make you laugh and humor is great fuel for the creative process.

A Word of Caution

There are times and situations in which, no matter how much work you put in personally, this multi-layered problem-solving model won't work. It is likely because of an attitude held by one party that may not be evident on the surface but is undermining the process. These issues include trying to collaborate with someone who feels entitled, lacks trust in you, is motivated by power and control, or is skillfully sabotaging. Intractable problems may be red flags for the presence of contempt and require the help of a third party. If your partner in life—the one who claims to love you the most—is intentionally obstructing a creative solution and increasing ongoing conflict, there are **very serious** problems in the relationship. People who truly love one another do not do this. Ever. Period.

Never underestimate the power of compromise, empathy, and brainstorming. Amy and her husband, Nick, have been guest speakers in my Psychology of Marriage class several times. During the Q&A portion of one of their talks, one student's question was, "What do you do when you just can't come to an agreement?" Nick immediately wanted to field this question and said, very simply, that if he and Amy got stuck in a disagreement, "I just decide to try it her way first. I trust her. I know she has our best interests in mind. I know she has a lot of knowledge and experience." In short, he is open to influence *(Skill No. 7: Accept Your Partner's Influence)* and makes a clear decision to compromise. *My students were shocked at the simplicity of this strategy.* The disagreement is no longer symbolic and there are no unconscious motives at play. I think of this as the clear recognition that **we are on the same team** as opposed to competing with one another. Problem-solving becomes much easier when this shift happens.

My hope is that when you get stuck, *and you will,* this model and these tips can help you either solve a problem or begin the work of uncovering what is underneath the impasse in your relationship.

LOVE Questions for Reflection and Discussion

Are you the kind of person who gets attached to one solution and then locks on to that? What strategies could you use to imagine multiple solutions to a problem? If you are struggling to come up with one, see the next question.

Who is the most creative person you know? Ask them how they solve problems or approach obstacles.

Many people feel discomfort when they are being asked to think outside the box. What are some of the ways you can handle your discomfort or anxiety when considering solutions that feel unfamiliar to you?

LOVE Checklist

☐ Identify a problem that needs a creative solution. First ask yourself, "Do I want this problem solved?" Next, with your partner, brainstorm a list of every possible solution the two of you can think of. If the situation is something children might be a part of, you could even include them in the brainstorming. Let the ideas flow and see what happens.

☐ Pay attention to when you are in cognitive or emotional lockdown. Give voice to your fears. Your needs. In what ways could you find more flexibility in thought and action?

☐ When there is a stuck place in a problem that needs to be solved, see if you can identify whether this is a structural, philosophical, or unconscious problem.

☐ If you are dealing with any trauma around any of the issues listed in the section *A Word of Caution*, we encourage you to seek professional help.

Love Resources

- *Think Again: The Power of Knowing What You Don't Know,* by Adam Grant

- *The Surprising Habits of Original Thinkers* TED Talk, Adam Grant

- Learn Assertiveness: mayoclinic.org/healthy-lifestyle/ stress-management/in-depth/assertive/art-20044644

This is perhaps the most practical aspect of your relationship.

Family, recreation, finances, and sex are areas that many couples struggle with in the day-to-day, ordinariness of life.

There's nothing fancy about the raw materials that give shape to these spaces in your relationship; these are the defining rooms in which you live.

But done poorly or without proper attention to detail, you might find yourself with a house—a relationship—that doesn't meet your needs.

Marriage is like a table with four legs—the couple, the children, the parents, and the in-laws. Break any of these and the marriage crashes to the floor.

—Siddharth Katragadda

Work with Your Partner's Family

by *Rhea*

Careful now. This is an area where feelings can get easily hurt. Even when not said out loud, there is often an unspoken line in the sand— *You can mess with me but don't mess with my family.*

You might be surprised to learn that couple's counselors have an understanding: Whenever a couple enters their office, there are really AT LEAST six people in the room—the couple, and both partner's mothers and fathers. If there are step-families, there are even more people in the room. The therapy room is VERY crowded! You *really* don't just marry your partner, you also marry their families.

Countless movies incorporate this theme. One of my favorites is *My Big Fat Greek Wedding* (2002), written by Nia Vardalos, who also starred in it. It shows what happens when two people from very different cultures fall in love and decide to marry. The reality of culture, however, is that ALL families have different *family* cultures, regardless of ethnicities, religion, country of origin, regional differences, or rural vs. urban orientations. The fact is that every family has differing practices, philosophies, traditions, values, and models for how a couple operates day-to-day and how they think about their "couplehood," despite any apparent similarities.

Problems arise when couples dismiss these differences as inconsequential to their relationship because ultimately, these differences are inescapable. We bring *who we are* into our relationships.

In the movie, Vardalos' character, Toula, meets a man, Ian (played by John Corbett) with whom she is immediately smitten. Ian is an only child, vegetarian, stoic, New England, protestant academic. Toula is, well, Greek. Her family owns a family restaurant, collaborates on some other local businesses, and mostly has not been to college. As the couple gets to know each other, Toula is wary of their obvious differences. "So you have two cousins and I have 27 first cousins. Just 27 first cousins alone, and my whole family is big and loud, and everyone is in each other's lives and business all the time." When Toula adds "No one has ever gone out with a non-Greek before, no one! And you're, well, wonderful. But I just don't see how this is going to work out," Ian says, "Work out? What's to work out? We're not a different species." But later in the movie, when his parents are introduced, one might think differently!

Toula has a good grasp on the potential problems even before meeting Ian's parents, although he seems a bit blind to the challenges. While these differences should not be considered deal-breakers, they are worthy of attention and discussion. Lots of discussion.

But most people don't even recognize the unique culture of their family. I had a rude awakening when I got married at 21. I don't remember much leading up to my aha-moment, but it came when I was cooking dinner. I got upset because I needed a certain type of pot with a certain type of utensil to make whatever it was. I was actually *very* upset—weepy and frustrated. See, in my family, there were a lot of specific rules about how to do things. More importantly, there was only one way. My husband's family, in contrast, were "make-doers"— just make do with whatever is available. When he asked me why I couldn't use another type of pot, I had no answer. My logical brain knew it would do but my family training said that wasn't the right type of pot. I heard the *ding, ding, ding* of awareness go off in my head. I too am now the Queen of Making-Do.

At a glance, our backgrounds appeared fairly similar: mostly Germanic heritage, Protestant Christians, three kids, Southern-born, middle class, nice parents. Not at all like the scenes in *My Big, Fat Greek Wedding*. While their differences were obvious, ours were not. But all families are different and the challenge in marriage is how to work with these family differences.

Have you seen *Father of the Bride*? After Steve Martin's character has a meltdown in the grocery store and ends up in jail, his wife (Diane Keaton) comes to bail him out. She suggests, "Don't you think you overreacted?" to his outburst. He replies simply, "I come from a long line of over-reactors!" Know what's in your own lineage so you can help your partner understand what lies ahead.

> *My feeling about in-laws was that they were outlaws.* —Malcolm X

It is not uncommon for a couple to encounter trouble when it comes to extended family. This is particularly the case at holidays, family vacations, weddings, and funerals—really anytime there is increased stress, unrealistic demands, and unconscious expectations. Similar to the mounting stress in *Father of the Bride*, unspoken expectations or differences of perspective will undoubtedly land a couple in conflict, either with each other, or with their families. Like so many issues a couple faces, empathy and good communication go a long way.

Six Guidelines for Working with Your Partner's Family

1. **The couple is the new family.** This rule is the first and most important guideline, and where each partner's loyalty should lie. You are in this together and the decisions about how you live your life together belong to you as a couple. This is the notion of "cleaving" to your partner in the marriage—to stick closely, loyally, and unwavering. Building your attachment as a couple and creating a marital identity is a foundational task in relationship formation. Have each other's back. Cleave.

2. **Advocate.** When dealing with your own family of origin (your parents, siblings, and extended family), you must be the one to speak directly to them—your family, your voice. In this way, you advocate for the needs of you and your life partner. It is also normal for families to feel misunderstood by the "outlaw" and it is your job to communicate about family traditions to your partner. You are the conduit for positive communication in both directions.

3. **Practice Acceptance.** Treat times with your partner's family as an adventure to another country. This is the world your partner grew up in and you have a rich opportunity to get an insider's view of your beloved and why they operate the way they do. Inasmuch as you can, approach this family as if you were a tourist: be polite, be curious, make attempts to speak their language, and at least try their food.

4. **Communicate, communicate, communicate.** First with your partner. Then with their family. What are the family rules for communication? What are the hot topics? Practice generous listening and engage with their stories to develop a deeper understanding of who they are. Get to know them through your own lens and not just those of your partner. Look for common ground.

5. **Practice good boundaries.** Boundaries may be around the length of the visit, where you stay—in their home or at a hotel, expectations, and personal preferences ahead of time. Boundaries may sound like, "You know, my partner, Alex, is an introvert and needs alone time so please don't be offended if they go to another room to take a time out." Or, "Jordan and I like to get out and explore when we're away from home, so we may take an afternoon to ourselves." And, "I'd like to take Taylor to some of my old haunts while we're here and to meet some of my old friends, so we're planning on going out a couple of evenings." Well-communicated boundaries can shift an interaction from misunderstanding and hurt feelings to a successfully navigated visit.

6. **Remember to breathe and to practice patience and empathy.** Remember that for good or bad, these are the people who shaped this person that you love. Managing differences in an expanding family is an evolving process. Some families have a harder time managing growing pains than other families. It is another aspect of familial cultural differences. Finding clear but subtle ways to manage unspoken forces can help people shift their perspectives. "Mom, we want to establish some of our own traditions as a married couple. How did you and dad do that? What was it like for you early in your marriage? How did you handle all the demands of the extended families?" Curiosity goes a long way in creating cross-cultural understandings.

Philosophical Differences

What if you and your partner disagree on how to handle extended families? These philosophical differences are some of the **hard conversations** *(Skill No. 13)* that couples need to have in advance of tough situations whenever possible, bearing in mind that it is often impossible to please everyone—especially when the demands are at cross-purposes. For example, a couple who agrees to spend holidays apart with their own families of origin find themselves caught in a situation where everyone's agenda cannot be satisfied. AND the parents are not supporting the sanctity of their kids' marriage with their dogged holiday demands. This is a couple who needs to claim their marital bond. It is a boundary that protects the relationship and deserves respect.

Families, your own and your partner's, are a vital facet of most of your lives. Don't think for a moment that they have no effect—the messages we learn are always stored deep within and we must learn to navigate those influences with our new partner. We all have a map from childhood about how to handle conflict, communicate affection, divide responsibilities, manage loyalties, divide time at holidays, and many, many others. Knowing yourself, communicating with your partner, and working with their family on a new model of an expanding family will always be the first steps that you'll need to repeat, time and time again.

LOVE Questions for Reflection and Discussion

How did you react to the opening paragraph's statement, "Couple's counselors have an understanding: Whenever a couple enters their office, there are really AT LEAST six people in the room—the couple, and both partners' mothers and fathers"?

Thinking back to Skill No. 5 *(Manage Your Boundaries)* on setting boundaries, what are the boundaries you and your partner need with your respective families? Have any of these required some creative problem-solving? What are the stuck places in dealing with your families?

What are some of the ways that you and your partner claim your relationship as your own family and as a priority? What tension arises in the face of competing demands and other family agendas?

LOVE Checklist

- ☐ Together, make a list of the strengths of each of your extended families. Make attempts to focus on these strengths and to draw upon them in your relationship.

- ☐ In one column, inventory things you and your partner see in your respective parents' marriages/relationships that you do not want to have as a part of your own relationship. In the second column, clarify how you alternately want your relationship to operate with specific behaviors and goals.

- ☐ Practice negotiations around holidays and special occasions. Set goals as a couple and strategize on how to manage those boundaries with your extended families.

LOVE Resources

- *How I Met Your Mother,* Season 7, Episode 7, "Noretta"

- *The Meaning of Marriage: Facing the Complexities of Commitment with the Wisdom of God,* by Timothy Keller

- *In-law Relationships: Mothers, Daughters, Fathers, and Sons,* by Geoffrey L. Grief and Michael E. Woolley

- psychologytoday.com/us/blog/lessons-loving/201611/3-rules-getting-along-your-in-laws?amp

Notes:

Your lovin' gives me such a thrill
But your lovin' don't pay the bills.

—lyrics to *Money (That's What I Want)*

Get On the Same Spreadsheet

by *Amy*

If working with your partner's family isn't hard enough, adding money management to the mix will surely give you a thrill!

According to recent research[1], money is one of the six areas couples fight about the most. I don't think this comes as a big surprise, but it is always comforting to know that research confirms our suspicions. But why is money such a difficult topic? Because money issues might be the stage where themes of dominance, transparency, control, and core values get acted out. There are also many emotions attached to money. And those are some BIG issues in a relationship!

Jesus did not shy away from the hard topic of money. Eleven of the 39 parables talk about the proper use of money or possessions. He warns repeatedly about the dangers of attachment to money, tells us what to do with our money, and mentors us about being generous with all our possessions—time, talent, spiritual gifts, as well as money. The Buddha had many teachings, too, about how to use money and possessions to help others. Money isn't good or evil; it is how a person uses or doesn't use money that creates the problem.

How you and your partner manage money can be as unique as your relationship. No one pattern works for everyone. However, there are a few key points that would be helpful for the two of you to discuss clearly—you know, to have those necessary hard conversations *(Skill No. 13)*! A Well's Fargo survey **found that happy couples talk more about money than unhappy couples**. I want you to be happy, so let's start talking.

Know And Share Your History. Try asking each other these questions: How was money dealt with in your family of origin? Were there separate checking accounts? Was there communal money? Were there "allowances"? How were the big purchases handled? How much money was given away and who got to decide where that money was given? Was there enough money? How much anxiety existed around the use of money? Were there secrets around money and spending? These questions help you to understand what was modeled for you and give you a way to bring to consciousness some of those patterns and emotions regarding money. This can be some complex inner work.

Know and Share Your Strengths and Weaknesses around Money. Have you always been a good budgeter? Or, does money seem to slip through your fingers? Are you an impulse buyer? Can you delay gratification—do you always pause and think twice about any purchase? Are you a repurposer? Do new things capture your interest more? Are you a visionary or more of a day-to-day kind of money manager? Is saving important to you? Or are you more of a *carpe diem* money human? Do you love to give gifts?

Know and Share Your Values. Do you value saving? Tithing? Do you feel compelled to help those less fortunate? Are you a public-school supporter, or is sending the kids to private school or boarding school important? How important are vacations? Traveling to see family? Saving for children's or grandchildren's college education? Are there issues, like climate change, responsibility to the planet, or sustainable living that will impact how you want to spend your money? Do you want full transparency around money? Or is having some money you do not have to account for important to you?

Would you both be willing to take care of family members who need things you can provide?

Once you have done that kind of sharing, which is more of a broad brushstroke, you can move into harder, more practical and detailed conversations. Here are some suggestions for handling conversations about money.

Set the Stage. As is true for any difficult or emotional conversation, set the stage. Don't have these conversations when you are hungry, angry or anxious, lonely, or tired (H.A.L.T.). Perhaps you and your partner need to have a money date—a time and place when you will both be able to attend completely to each other and the issues at hand. Get a babysitter if necessary. Turn off the screens. Be free of any other distractions.

Start Slowly and Positively. It is okay to acknowledge that the conversation may feel awkward and difficult at first. You may want to start with the things that are going well. What do you see your partner doing well? When has the use of money brought you happiness and joy? Also, if you know you have been at fault about some things, it is helpful to take responsibility and admit that. "I know I overspent last month on clothes. I can do better." Or, "I know I said I would ask you before I made a big purchase and I know that is upsetting to you."

Find Common Ground. If you both want to invest in your garden, then talk about the money that will be necessary to do that. If you both want to go visit friends, then talk about the way you can save to make that happen. Coming together around some joint ventures is a helpful way to ease the tension.

Look at the Numbers. This can be the hardest part but as I always say to my family and my clients, "I can deal with anything, as long as it is the truth." Digital banking makes it quite easy to look at the numbers. Most banks will show you a graph depicting what you are spending in different categories. It can be shocking to see how much groceries cost. Or how much you spent on fast-food or specialty coffee. Yikes. Or, add up those fees for Netflix, Apple TV, Hulu, Disney+, and Amazon Prime. It may shock you. Your pets are costing you how much? Is there really money in the budget for all those leisurely things you want to do, or is that taxing the budget to a breaking point?

Do Some Dreaming. It can be helpful to have some future focus when money is a stressor. If you both really want something, whatever it is, find a way to save for it. Even if it means putting a few dollars a week into a fund, it can feel satisfying to have a joint dream you are working toward.

Stick with It. Remember, happy couples talk about money more often than unhappy couples. Once money is no longer a taboo topic, you can find ways to work together to everyone's satisfaction.

I often talk about money as energy. If money is managed well, there is a sense of freedom in us. If money is out in the open, without deceit, most issues can be dealt with. Money will not buy you happiness. It will buy you choices. So learning how to successfully navigate the financial realm of your relationship will keep good energy flowing and keep the bond between you in good shape. Money issues can indeed be messy. Sometimes they can sink the marriage ship. Don't let that happen to you.

And just for fun, here are **my top ten favorite songs about money**. You know if there is music about it there is a universality to the theme. You are not alone!

- 💜 *Money (That's What I Want)*, Barrett Strong (original), and later The Beatles
- 💜 *For The Love of Money*, The O'Jay's
- 💜 *Money*, Pink Floyd

- *Money, Money, Money,* ABBA
- *Money, Honey,* Clyde McPhatter and the Drifters
- *Money Changes Everything,* Cyndi Lauper
- *She Works Hard for the Money,* Donna Summer
- *Take the Money and Run,:* The Steve Miller Band
- *You Never Give Me Your Money,* The Beatles
- *Lawyers, Guns, and Money,* Warren Zevon

LOVE Questions for Reflection and Discussion

How do you honestly feel about sharing your thoughts and beliefs about money? It's a scary topic for many, and therefore is often avoided. So be as transparent as you can about this question.

If you went to bed tonight and woke up tomorrow morning and had won the $10 million-dollar lottery, what would you do with the money? Discuss this with your partner.

This skill is already FULL of questions for your discussion. Go back through this one and use the questions as conversation starters.

LOVE Checklist

☐ For at least 30 days, or maybe for 60 or 90, keep a detailed accounting of every penny you spend. You can do this in a notebook or journal, or on your phone. However you do it, be absolutely accurate. At the end of those days, tally up how you spend your money, in themes. For instance, groceries, recreation, health and wellness, children, travel, medical, home expenses, etc.

☐ If you and/or your partner are in financial trouble, do not hesitate to seek help. Admitting you need help figuring things out or getting out of financial trouble is the first step to taking control of this part of your life. There are public agencies that help people with debt consolidation and also private individuals who work to help individuals and couples with financial problems.

☐ Complete the *Autobiography of Money* on the next two pages.

LOVE Resources

It's Not about the Money, by Brett Kessler

See the *Autobiography of Money* on pages 108–109

psychologytoday.com/us/blog/experimentations/
201912/30-core-disagreements-couples-encounter

Footnote

1. sciencedirect.com/science/article/abs/pii/
    S0191886919306750?via%3Dihub

Autobiography of Money

If you google "Autobiography of Money," you will find about a dozen sources. Most of these questions are used with permission from Richard B. Wagner's work as the Director of the Integral Finance Center. I have also added a few of my own questions to the mix. Good luck!

- What is your earliest memory of money? Your happiest memory? Your unhappiest?

- What is your earliest memory of having your own money, whether that was getting an allowance, or getting money for your birthday or Christmas. Were you coached about how to use this money? For instance, were you encouraged to give money away or save money? Is this a happy memory or an unhappy one?

- How was the subject of money addressed in your home? In other words, how did your family communicate about money?

- How did your mother address money? Your father?

- How money was managed in your home? By whom?

- Were there fights about money? Secrets about how money was spent?

- What or who was the primary source of money for you as a child?

- How did your church or religious institution talk about money?

- How were you confronted with the knowledge of differing economic circumstances among people, that there were people "richer" or "poorer" than you?

- Growing up, did you feel rich or poor?

- Were you ever anxious about money as a child?

- When did you first acquire a credit card?

- What did it represent to you?

- Do you have debt now? How do you feel about debt?

- Have your attitudes about money shifted during your adult life?

- Are you money motivated?

- Are you financially fearful or resentful?

- If you are partnered, how did the two of you decide how to manage your money? For instance, did you do it the way you did growing up? Did you want something different?

- Do you feel financially safe in your partnership? Why or why not? What would help you feel safe?

- Are you generous or stingy with money? Do you give gifts? Tip?

- How much money do you give away in a year? Calculate this as a percentage of your take-home income.

- What part does money play in your spiritual life?

- What are the possible threats to your income?

- Do you have a contingency plan in the event your income is disrupted for any reason?

- Do you know your net worth?

- Do you have insurance sufficient to meet anticipatable, foreseeable, not easily absorbable risks?

- Do you have a will?

- Have you ever examined your spending habits/patterns? Why or why not?

- Do you think you live your money values?

- Will you inherit money? How does this affect your attitude and habits toward money?

There are many more questions you can ask yourself about money. Just let these questions guide you and add anything more that feels important. Doing this with your partner can truly help you understand and communicate about this difficult yet necessary topic.

The more you invest in fun and friendship and being there for your partner, the happier the relationship will get over time.

—Howard Markman, PhD, University of Denver Center for
   Marital and Family Studies

Play and Laugh Together

by *Rhea*

After dealing with each other's families and money—you need a break! You deserve some fun and laughter in this serious business of building a life together.

It's a Hollywood trope: Protagonist is chasing after an appealing romantic partner while the best friend stands by trying to advise but secretly pining after Protagonist. The appealing romantic partner ends up not being so appealing and the best friends end up together because they know how to laugh and have fun together.

Very simply, playing and laughing together connects people and can offer a protective factor against boredom and disconnection. Distance in a relationship is the ultimate killer. Fostering closeness through play and playfulness can be part of the antidote.

Psychologist Arthur Aron and his colleagues at the University of New York at Stony Brook checked out this theory by having couples engage in silly, playful tasks. They then measured their levels of happiness in their relationship. This was compared to couples who engaged in a boring, mundane activity. The finding was significant, leading Aron and his colleagues to conclude that couples who participate in novel, exciting activities are brought together through cooperation and a shared experience.[1]

We don't stop playing because we grow old;
we grow old because we stop playing.
—George Bernard Shaw

Sadly, many adults believe play is a thing of childhood. When I was in college, I worked at a local hospital that brought in a consultant whose goal was to improve workplace morale. She focused largely on the importance of continuing to play as an adult. I remember thinking how intuitively OBVIOUS that was and wondering how I could get paid for that kind of job! Her point was that play improves peoples' overall sense of well-being but that many adults misunderstand what it means to play. Many people think of playing as a tennis match or any other competitive sport, but that's not really how *play* is defined.

Stuart Brown, psychiatrist, author (*Play*, 2009), researcher, and founder of the National Institute for Play, defines play as "a state of being that is purposeless, fun, and pleasurable." Playing a competitive sport has a goal. Authentic play is not goal-directed but focuses on the overall experience. Furthermore, Brown says play is not a trivial matter but is necessary for healthy development. He stumbled across the significance of play when researching the life stories and personality characteristics of murderers in a Texas prison and found that their childhoods lacked play. Moreover, Brown later found that creative, successful people have rich play lives.

Similarly, laughter may be overlooked as a vital part of life. Research has investigated what happens when we laugh (muscle contractions that promote deep breathing patterns and the subsequent release of endorphins), and it has clearly shown us *how* we benefit from laughter (increases pain tolerance, decreases the consequences of stress, and offsets the impact of negative affect and tension). But why we developed laughter as a species is more elusive.

Laughter is both social and contagious. We first begin to laugh as infants as young as about three months as one of our first preverbal ways of interacting with others. According to Robert R. Provine, psychologist and neuroscientist, and author of *Laughter* (2000), it is deemed contagious because even the sound of laughter can make us laugh. Have you ever broken out in uncontrollable giggles when you heard someone else start giggling?

Laughter fosters closeness and promotes social bonding. Robin Dunbar, an evolutionary psychologist from Oxford, believes laughter smoothes out barriers when interactions are intense or conflictual. This was important in social evolution as groups grew in complexity[2]. John Gottman confirms that humor is an important tool in managing conflict in relationships.

So it appears that if we play and laugh with the people we love, we will develop more positive associations in that relationship. Positive memories, even in the face of hardship, help us create meaning in our lives.

That positive, warm, humorous spin on events also helps us maintain perspective. All of these researchers came to the same conclusion: playing together helps couples to rebuild emotional intimacy in their relationships. I saw this play out during a professional trip to Italy. One of our colleagues recognized the night before leaving that his wife's passport had expired. With a lot of scrambling, money, and a delayed departure, alone and two days behind the group, she finally arrived. Her frustration with her husband was layered in humor and it quickly made for a great story as our mantra on the trip became *tragedy + time = comedy*. Laughing at these kinds of debacles can help repair hard feelings.

Play and laughter bring joy and bond people. Most of us could use more joy and bonding. There are plenty of "checkbooks and toilets" (as a client once said) in our relational lives—issues that often disgruntle and divide us. In fact, it's easy to get stuck in the business of life; but keep in mind that play and laughter are very important business in our emotional lives. As Brown succinctly says, **"Play is the purest expression of love."**

This skill is simple and straightforward. Remember, all work and no play makes us dull. We become bored with ourselves, bored with our lives, and then likely looking at our partner and thinking they're boring too. Novel, exciting, cooperative activities are corrective emotional experiences that connect us. These are the marvelous experiences we can laugh about in the story of our shared lives.

LOVE Questions for Reflection and Discussion

What is play for you?

Play is also very creative. What are the ways you are creative in your play?

How do you make yourself laugh? How does your partner make you laugh?

LOVE Checklist

☐ Make a list of the ways you and your partner can play together. Hang it in an obvious place and pick one of the things to do at least once a week.

☐ Try playing in a completely new way. It may fail, and that is okay, but it may be surprising and add life to your relationship.

☐ How often do you and your partner laugh together? Make it a point to share laughter at least once a day.

LOVE Resources

Play: How It Shapes the Brain, Opens the Imagination, and Invigorates the Soul, by Stuart Brown

Play Is More Than Just Fun TED Talk, Stuart Brown

Laughter: A Scientific Investigation, by Robert R. Provine

Couples Who Play Together Stay Together, https://psych-your-mind.blogspot.com/2012/01/psychology-says-couples-who-play.html?m=1

Footnotes

1. Aron, A. Norman, C., Aron, E., McKenna, C., & Heyman, R. (2000). Couples' shared participation in novel and arousing activities and experienced relationship quality. *Journal of Personality and Social Psychology, 78*(2), 273-284.

2. nytimes.com/2011/09/14/science/14laughter.html?_r=0

Notes:

I have no objection to anyone's sex life as long as they don't practice it in the street and frighten the horses.

—Oscar Wilde

Do It

by *Rhea*

Speaking of fun ...

We're breaking form on this one and we've invited the input of one of our treasured friends and colleagues, Dr. Sarah E. Wright, a licensed psychologist. So what has Sarah got that we don't? Well, she is also a certified sex therapist. And because of her area of expertise, we thought it would be interesting to get her input *(Skill No. 14: Ask for Help)* since she has so much experience poking around in other people's sex lives. We also thought a little sexual innuendo in this chapter would be fun!

Let's start at the very beginning. ... The following is our version of Dr. Sarah's list of Good Sex Guidelines.

- 💜 **Everyone is responsible for safe and healthy practices.** The health and well-being of your partner, and ultimately, your relationship depend on it. This applies to both STIs or pregnancy prevention. Don't make assumptions or skip important conversations, regardless of your sexual orientation or gender identity. Not to sound like your 7th-grade health teacher, but you are responsible for using protection and being prepared. Always.

- 💜 **Set personal limits/boundaries and share them.** It is worth emphasizing that your boundaries and limits need to be discussed so that you are both on the same page. These discussions can also serve to help you develop and maintain emotional closeness. For example, "I really prefer afternoon sex when I'm not so tired, like on Friday nights." Or consider this important conversation: "I prefer that you tell me what you're going to do before making any quick moves. My molester from my early teens always took me by surprise and that makes me scared. I'm not scared of you—and I don't want to develop any fear between us."

💜 **Talk about sex.** One hangover from Victorian and Puritan cultures, particularly in the U.S., is a hang-up around talking about sex. Many conversations about sex revolve around some aspects: how not to do it, rigid moralistic rules about when/where/how/and with whom, or how to prevent disease or pregnancy. But how often do parents and teens/young adults talk about the benefits of sex or pleasure? It is rare that those conversations are a part of what we call "sex education." But let's face it, most people have sex for the sheer pleasure and the connection it builds. For example, did you know that the clitoris is the only organ whose sole purpose is pleasure? Pretty cool fun fact, huh?

So how do we learn about these aspects of sex? Movies? Peers in adolescence? Porn? These are less than adequate. What about you and your partner? To know and understand each other and how you're doing as a couple, you are going to need to talk about sex. Two suggestions:

1. **Talk outside the bedroom.** Because this is such an important aspect of couples' lives, it is worth doing well. Naked, in bed, before or after sex, leaves us feeling particularly vulnerable. Talking about sex in those moments can add more pressure. We really want to be in a position to reduce pressure when having potentially hard conversations *(Skill No. 13)*.

2. **Plan for talking about sex.** Sometimes the time to strike is NOT when the iron is hot. Set a time to talk if necessary.

♥ **Know yourself.** You are largely responsible for your own pleasure. This may be a novel idea, so let's break it down. If you don't know what is pleasurable to you, how is your partner supposed to decipher this? Of course there are physiological cues, but those can be misunderstood. For example, you might jump in reaction to a type of touch, and that could be interpreted either as (bad) pain, meaning "don't do that anymore," or super (good) sensitivity which may then communicate "go back there again." So know yourself and then:

♥ **Send clear messages.** When most of our rational brain is offline and we are immersed in the experience of sex, it is easy to miscommunicate. As a result, partners can all too easily feel hurt, blamed, or misunderstood. Here are two easy skills to practice which can lubricate these interactions so they go more smoothly.

1. **Use I statements.** The basic formula, "**I feel _____ when _____**" makes it harder for your partner to feel blamed or shamed about what they're doing because you are taking responsibility for your feelings *(Skill No. 15: Learn to Fight, Rule #1)*. In sex, the difference might be like this: "I feel especially close to you when we enjoy long kisses after orgasm." vs. "You don't kiss me much after sex—you act like you're just ready to be done." These are very different messages!

2. **Use positive language.** Ask for what you want rather than what you don't want. If you say, "don't do that," or "that hurts," your partner will likely be unsure what to do next. Instead, try saying, "I like it when you do that slower." or, "Do it like this." and then guide your partner. It's like the old "Don't think of a pink elephant"; now all you have in your mind is a pink elephant rather than what you need to focus on. Turn your Don'ts into Do's!

- **Broaden your definition of sex.** Intercourse? Orgasm? Foreplay? How about afterplay? What about a friendly game of kissing, touching, and teasing in the kitchen? Or have you thought about sex as lying in bed and simply touching? Probably not. We tend to think about sex as the act of intercourse that ends with orgasm. That is a very patriarchal, heteronormative, limiting definition. Wouldn't it remove some of the performance pressure if we weren't always so performance oriented? YES! And it allows us to relax into all things pleasurable. So let's not cut this wonderful experience short with a narrow definition.

- **It's Okay to say "No."** For good or bad, depending upon which side of the equation you're on, the NO's win. Always. "No" means no and "Stop" means stop. This is about personal boundaries and consent. Respecting your partner means respecting their sexual boundaries. Even if you initially say "yes" you retain the right to change that to a "no" at any point. This is best illustrated in the Tea Consent video available on YouTube: (https://youtu.be/oQbei5JGiT8). Simple, eloquent, and clear.

- **Rejection of sex is not rejection of you.** We are all complicated humans. Sometimes we're not in the mood. Sometimes we have competing goals in our heads and don't feel available for sex. Other times, we may be feeling emotions that are interfering with engaging sexually. We may simply be too tired. And, believe it or not, sometimes a headache is just a headache.

- **Be creative with safety.** Many people are very adventurous in their sex lives. It's fine to explore the edges of pain, roles, or fantasy as long as each person is in agreement about physical and emotional safety. Communication is the key. Discuss your boundaries and, yes, people actually DO use safe words, like "stop," "no more," or, "I don't like that."

💜 **Masturbate.** Despite how this may have been treated in your childhood, masturbation is a healthy practice. Our sexual organs work on the same principle as other muscles: Use it or lose it. Also, masturbation is one of the best ways to explore your own body and to understand your pleasure centers. And if you're male-bodied, daily masturbation can reduce your risk of prostate cancer (another fun fact). Contrary to Puritan lore, you won't go blind!

I would add one more thing to Dr. Sarah's list:

💜 **Be intentional about entering your partner's world.** That effort to connect with them in the way they want to be connected with, touched, and loved goes a long way to communicate **"I value you."** "I see you. I hear you. I understand you. And I am willing to meet you where you are." Twice in the 1990s, I saw comedian Rob Becker's brilliant one-man show, *Defending the Caveman,* and this is the thrust of his message. He emphasizes that neither party in a couple is wrong nor right, but we each approach relationships from our own perspective. He enacted this in a sexual scene with his wife:

Her: (behind him massaging his ears and cooing): *Honey, doesn't this just feel so good?*

Him: (trying not to be impatient): *It would feel a lot better two feet lower on the other side.*

So meet your partner where they are and just do it!

LOVE Questions for Reflection and Discussion

What messages did you get in your family or culture regarding sex? How have these messages shaped how you feel today about sex?

Have you ever been the victim of a sexual assault? Does your partner know about this? How does this affect the way you approach your sexual relationships?

What is your sexual IQ? How much do you know about your own body, your own desires and preferences? How willing are you to learn about your partner's body and desires? How comfortable are you expressing your desires?

How comfortable are you expressing sexual boundaries? Are you partnered with someone who respects those?

LOVE Checklist

☐ Get familiar with your own body. Know what you find pleasurable and what you don't. Know what gets in your way when you are with another person.

☐ A lasting and satisfying sex life takes time, energy, and devotion. Make sure you and your partner are setting aside time and energy for this important aspect of your relationship.

☐ Talk with your partner about sex. Do it. Have the hard conversations *(Skill No. 13)* that you might be avoiding.

LOVE Resources

Mating in Captivity: Unlocking Erotic Intelligence, by Esther Perel

Where Do We Begin Podcast, Esther Perel

Sex Points: Reclaim Your Sex Life with the Revolutionary Multi-Point System, by Bat Sheva Marcus

Please read Dr. Sarah E. Wright's thoughtful book, *Redefining Trauma: Understanding and Coping with a Cortisoaked Brain* (Routledge Press, 2020). It is amazing and she is a Rock Star!

Notes:

Stage Four: Unexpected Setbacks

A flawlessly executed building project is a myth. It just doesn't happen.

There are always setbacks: damaged materials, unexpected and uncontrollable time delays, problems with foundations and framing that have been covered up, miscommunications of all kinds. The reasons for setbacks are as unique and numerous as the projects themselves.

A perfect union is also a myth. There will always be messes in life that demand our ability and willingness to communicate well, to have a healthy fight if necessary, and to learn to apologize.

Master partners, like master builders, don't abandon ship when they encounter problems, but skillfully navigate their way toward more solid footing.

We don't live in a shared reality, we each live in a reality of our own, and causing upset is often the price of trying to reach each other. It is always easier to dismiss other people than go through the awkward and time-consuming process of understanding them.

—Frankie Boyle

Have the Hard Conversations

by

It is a natural part of any relationship to have setbacks, and it is equally natural to want to avoid conflict. However, please know that one hard conversation can be the thing that transforms us. We are afraid. We don't want to make things worse. And if we don't have the skills, we are pretty sure that having a hard conversation badly is not good either.

An intake with a client went something like this:

Me: Why do you think your marriage ended?

Client: Well, in the end, I had an affair.

Me: Is that what broke up the marriage?

Client: What broke up the marriage was the fact that we never had a hard conversation. We both hated conflict and we avoided it. We had a nice home, raised the kids, worked too hard, and basically stayed away from anything hard. Including the topic of sex. I cracked where we were the weakest.

Me: Sex was where you were the weakest?

Client: Nope. I was the weakest at having hard conversations.

Couples need to have hard conversations, and yet they may not have the skills and therefore lack confidence, fear hurting their partner's feelings, or want to be "nice" (ugh). Or, they have some trauma around conflict that rears its head whenever they think about disagreements. When conflict gets swept under the proverbial rug, it isn't gone. Instead, it festers, causing emotional pain and regret, lack of respect, and sometimes the dreaded and often relationship-ending feeling of contempt.

I mentioned earlier in this book the father/son team of psychiatrists, Tom and Pat Malone. The paradigm they offer of a loving relationship as a combination of closeness and intimacy is helpful when learning to have hard conversations. You might remember that *closeness* is mostly about the details of life together. **Intimacy,** by their definition, is the state of being where one person can be completely who they are in the other's presence, and vice versa. Most hard conversations are about intimacy, and might sound like this: *I need you to know something about me. I need to share feelings that may seem irrational to you but are important to me. I am afraid that what I am going to say is going to hurt you, and it might, but my intention is to make things better, to make our relationship more real, more honest.*

Here are a few tips for having hard conversations.

Lean in. Virginia Satir left a legacy of helpful tools for marriages, families, and communities. One of these tools is a formula for having difficult (and maybe most) conversations; she called it the Temperature Reading. Here are the four parts.

1. **Appreciations.** Name something(s) about your partner you honestly appreciate and for which you are grateful. These can be behaviors, core values, or recent efforts.

2. **Bugs or puzzles, and possible solutions.** What is the problem and how can we solve it? What is not going so well? Can we do some problem-solving that will make this easier? Virginia also said there are always three possible solutions to a problem: yours, mine, and the ones we haven't thought of yet.

3. **New information.** Is there anything we have not talked about yet? Anything pending that is important?

4. **Hopes and wishes.** What are the unspoken dreams? What do you hope will happen and when?

Listen/be curious. Listen with your eyes, ears, heart, and body. What do you see in your partner? Fear? Yearning? Exhaustion? Where do you see it? Do her eyes always look a certain way when she is tired or sick? Do his cheeks flush when he feels frustrated or angry? Does he talk faster when he is anxious? What unlived dreams are just beneath the surface that if room were made for them would have an immense impact on the quality of the marriage? Try approaching these conversations with a deep curiosity. What can I learn about my partner that would help us get to the bottom of a problem?

Schedule family meetings. One way to practice having hard conversations is to schedule family or partner meetings. These can be weekly, although my experience is that most people are so busy that weekly can seem like too much. So maybe bi-weekly or monthly would be enough? Use these meetings to practice the Temperature Reading. When you are doing this, try approaching each meeting with sincerity and curiosity. What will I learn about my partner? Can I be a good detective and get to the bottom of a problem? Can I learn to be a better question asker?

Stay connected to your core values. If honesty is a core value for you, say it, mean it, and practice it. Feeling betrayed by secrets, denial, or covert information could eventually lead to trouble. If staying connected to extended family is important to you, hold fast. It is worth the rumble to figure out how to engage with family, what the boundaries are, what to do if extended family is difficult, and what the long-term goals are. You get the idea.

Allow for silence. Sometimes during hard conversations we just need to sit with each other a little—let what has been said settle in. Wonder about it. Sometimes we need to just breathe a little, feel what we are feeling, and come back to the conversation with some new realizations. This is important. Time for silence and assimilation can turn a tense and rigid conversation around into something softer and more organic. It's okay to say, "Let's just sit here and be quiet together for a few minutes and see what comes up." Another benefit of silence is that as it slows down the process, it usually lessens emotional flooding and impulsivity.

Stay focused on the entity of the relationship. The goal in any hard conversation should be the betterment of the relationship. Notice I did not say the goal is winning. Or proving how right you are. Or anything that has to do with you as an individual. The goal is to become more deeply connected to the other person, to feel more deeply understood, and to find ways to move forward that serve the relationship. Do you want to be right or do you want to be in a relationship (Yes, I am repeating this again!)? Keep this question front and center.

It's okay to ask for help with hard conversations. It's okay to want to have them in a therapist's office, or a minister's office. If you did not have a good model for these types of conversations, you are likely to need help. This is a skill that is built with years of practice. So don't avoid and don't shame yourself. Lean in to the messy of it, but know that when hard conversation goes well, it can be the most marvelous thing in your relationship. A true sense of accomplishment can follow, and a sense of pride in the relationship. "Look what we can do! We can do the hard stuff. Yay us!"

LOVE Questions for Reflection and Discussion

What models did you have growing up for having difficult conversations? Were they encouraged or discouraged in your family?

Recall the hardest conversation you have ever had. What made it so? What were your dominant emotions and how did you handle them?

If you are avoiding a hard conversation, where could you turn for help? Do you have a best friend, pastor, or therapist who could help you navigate a way to lean in to this conversation?

LOVE Checklist

☐ Using Virginia Satir's Temperature Reading model, have a conversation with your partner about a difficult subject. See how it goes.

☐ The best way to show up for a hard conversation is vulnerably and authentically. Practice those communication skills, use I-statements, and give yourself plenty of space to listen actively and to respond with care.

☐ Begin with the end in mind. This is the first habit from Stephen Covey's *The 7 Habits of Highly Effective People.* How do you want this conversation to end? Do you want it to end positively? Then start that way and stay focused in that direction. Do you want some specific changes made or to be understood in a specific way? Then start by saying that.

LOVE Resources

- *The Art of Intimacy,* by Tom and Pat Malone

- All of the Gottman books on marriage will have some sections on conversations and how to have them.

- *Difficult Conversations: Practical Tactics for Crucial Conversation,* by Joel A. Garfinkle

- Search the TED Talk website. Use Difficult Conversations as your search topic and you will have close to a dozen to choose from.

Notes:

Regardless of what challenge you are facing right now, know that it has not come to stay, it has come to pass. During these times, do what you can with what you have, and ask for help if needed.

—Les Brown

Ask for Help

by *Rhea*

Fans of the popular show, *This Is Us*, love it because the characters are real, complex, and flawed. These same characters have also destigmatized asking for help as we have watched the deeply personal struggles of siblings Randall, Kevin, Kate, her husband, Toby, and mother Rebecca. In fact, all of the family have been to treatment, rehab, or self-help groups, and they have even been to family therapy together. Imperfect, loveable, and heart-warming, everyone in this fictional family has asked for help. But ... it's fiction. ...

What is it about this skill? Why are we so reluctant to ask for help in the personal parts of our lives? As you know, we ask for help from our mechanics, the IT folks, a physician, a plumber, or a decorator. We even seek the help of a wedding planner. So why would we not ask for help when it comes to a relationship and the 1–70+ years that might *follow* the wedding day?

Relationships are complicated—at best. We try to take two incredibly different people from different backgrounds and families, ask them to live in close quarters and collaborate on every aspect of their lives, and then just say, *Good luck. Hope you make it!* ... For the rest of their lives. And we wonder why only about half of marriages make it to 40 years.

We don't get adequate training in long-term relationships. It is not taught in middle school—as one of my students suggested—before we start diving into romantic relationships. The only apprenticeships are in our own families of origin, and then about half of us had parents who were divorced. Hmmm ... sounds like a recipe for disaster. In fact, a failing marriage is one of the most intimately painful experiences one can have. The decision to marry is one of the few decisions we make with costly consequences if we change our minds.

According to the Gottmans' research, most couples suffer unhappiness and loneliness in a relationship for an average of six years before they seek help. I've had couples who said they should have come the first year they got married—over 10 years ago—because they recognized they had serious problems. The biggest problem with waiting six, 10, or 20 years is that the patterns of dysfunction become a part of the bones of the marriage. The relationship becomes distorted over time. Then, *finally*, when couples DO reach out, they typically want a quick and painless fix. In the first session, at least one will invariably ask, "How long will this take?" And the answer is, "How long have you been struggling?" So, *can* you wait too long? Sure, if one or both are done; however, if you're willing to work to salvage the relationship, transformation is almost always possible.

What are the warning signs that a relationship needs help? When:

- there is increasing or escalating conflict.
- your partner is not taking your concerns seriously or doesn't "have your back."
- there is growing distance in your level of intimacy (emotionally, sexually).
- you feel unsupported, dismissed, or devalued.
- there is betrayal (sexually, financially, emotionally).
- there is a serious external crisis that impairs your ability to function (illness, death, trauma, significant loss).

💜 there is abuse, addiction, and/or persistent mental illness.

💜 there is bullying, manipulation, or undermining control.

💜 you begin to have thoughts about getting out of the relationship.

Maybe one of the reasons we are reluctant to ask for help in our relationships is that we are afraid to admit that we might be wrong, that our version of things is merely "the story I tell myself." In fact, many couples come to therapy expecting the counselor to play judge and jury, to tell the other partner that they are wrong. Because relationships are about the most personal aspect of our lives, they are tangled up in our identity. Looking deeply at who we are in the mirror of our relationships takes extraordinary honesty, courage, humility, and vulnerability. This is *hard* work. But it is profitable work. And cheaper than a divorce.

I urge you not to wait for a crisis to shove you into asking for help. Psychiatrist Dr. George Blair-West, in his 2017 TEDxBrisbane talk, advocates for preventative medicine in a marriage, much like we do for any other public health problem; in other words, vaccinate yourself against marital problems. Preventative medicine or help can come in the form of premarital counseling. Counselors, some ministers, and reputable relationship coaches are going to bring up the hard topics that we don't want to talk about. Let's face it, when all is blissful, who wants to discuss something that could be potentially controversial? Most of us are rather conflict-avoidant. The idea that "we'll cross that bridge when we get there" is fodder for future conflict. After all, we do say *love is blind*, right?

When we have done our very, very best, papa, and that is not enough, then I think the right time must have come for asking the help of others.
—Charles Dickens in *Holiday Romance*

What can premarital counseling offer a couple? Just like any counseling, it is an objective set of eyes to reflect certain things you might have overlooked. No one would think of buying a house without a home inspection first. "But I just *love* this house!" Okay. Meanwhile, the plumbing under the central hallway is just pouring out under the house, creating hazardous mold and rotting wood. Furthermore, you don't take on the chore of crawling under the house to examine everything. *You ask for help.*

If you're well into your relationship, can therapy help? Yes. Most people want to solve their own problems, and if they could, they would. But sometimes couples just can't see clearly what keeps them stuck. Couple's counselors are specifically trained to untangle these messes by looking beneath the surface at deeper issues that may be covered up by the same old fight.

We used to say that marriages (or children) did not come with owner's manuals but that is simply not true today. We are living in the age of information, good information, at the tip of our fingers. Literally. We will list some of our favorite resources at the end of this chapter. Use them. Start early. Do your own research.

By now, if you've read other works by Messy Marvelous, you might notice a pattern. This skill, **Ask For Help**, was the first in our blog started in May 2015, and the first skill in our first book, *Launch: A Guide to Adulting*. Regarded as a high priority, it is a meta-skill—an overarching skill—that can be applied to many areas of our lives. Without asking for help, people are limited by what they already know. And if you knew what would help, surely you would have already fixed the problems you're struggling with in your relationship. Don't let fear or shame prevent you from having a successful relationship. Be brave. Ask for help.

LOVE Questions for Reflection and Discussion

If you think your relationship has needed help but you have not gotten it yet, what has prevented you from seeking assistance?

What were the sticking points in your parent's marriage? Were they able to ask for help?

Did you see them resolve problems? If not, what/who do you use as a model to resolve marital issues?

Do you have any friends who are in couple's counseling? Are conversations about this open and welcome or are they taboo? Would you hide it if you were in counseling or would you be open about it?

LOVE Checklist

☐ Take a yearly relationship inventory about things that are working well and areas that need improvement. Use this to consider whether you are on track or need help. If there is a repeated weak area, that may be a signal that help is needed.

☐ If one of you wants to go to counseling and the other doesn't, consider going on your own. Sometimes if one person changes a marriage can change, or at least the interactions can change.

☐ Vaccinate yourself against this allergy to dealing with difficult topics. Be brave, step forward, tackle the hard topics in small doses, and get the help you need.

LOVE Resources

Time for couples counseling? gottman.com/blog/
is-it-time-to-go-to-couples-counseling/

Ask for help in your marriage. psychologytoday.com/us/blog/
the-love-doctor/201012/5-ways-ask-help?amp

Great tips on how to ask for help: *How to ask for help—and get a "yes"* TED Salon, Dr. Heidi Grant, social psychologist

Marital conflict prevention: *Three ways to build a happy marriage and avoid divorce*, TEDxBrisbane, Dr. George Blair-West, psychiatrist

Notes:

If you can't go back to your mother's womb, you'd better learn to be a good fighter!

—Anchee Min

Learn to Fight

by *Rhea*

I blame many relationship ills on reality TV. The Real Housewives aren't very real, and *The Bachelor* franchise makes millions showcasing unrealistic relationships. In these types of shows, we see the "winners" look at the camera and deliver harsh criticisms of others without examining their part in the conflicts, spew unedited nastiness at one another, and punch below the belt. Does anyone know how to fight fairly? Perhaps not, as these examples make it easy to see that many people lack good conflict management skills.

There was a time in couples counseling when the predominant thinking was that if we could just decrease the amount of conflict in the relationship, we could save more marriages. Over time, we've learned that this is just not true. *Conflict is inevitable.* People we call "the Bickersons," who have ongoing low levels of arguing, don't necessarily part ways more often than couples with lower levels of conflict.

If you Google the term "fair fighting," you'll find all kinds of lists that tend to have many of the same guidelines. These have been well-established, not only by science, but arguably, by good sense. These are also considered generally effective communication guidelines that apply to other family relationships, friendships, and work relationships.

From this collective wisdom, I have culled my own list of 12 Fair-Fighting Rules. It is not intended to be exhaustive, but if you practice these, your problem-solving skills will get better and, more importantly, you will avoid further damaging your relationship.

1. **Take responsibility for yourself.** If you choose only one skill to practice, this one is potentially a game changer. Most people start their complaints with "YOU." Close your eyes for a minute and imagine trying to solve a problem with someone who is pointing at you and saying over and over, "YOU did this. YOU didn't do that. YOU. YOU. YOU." When I imagine this, I feel very lonely and hopeless. Being blamed is demoralizing and demeaning.

   The best strategy for taking responsibility for yourself is referred to as "*I statements*" and is considered Communication 101. It is structured like this:

   I feel *(insert emotion)* **when** *(insert situation)*.

   Try it. I would almost put money on the fact that you didn't use an emotion word after *I feel*, but rather a thought or judgment. Often it comes out as, "I feel *like you* _____." That is not a feeling or an emotion, and definitely doesn't reflect your own state. Interactions will go much more smoothly when each person takes responsibility for their own communication, emotional life, and perspective on their circumstances. It moves us from accusing and blaming to collaboration and connection.

2. **Attack the problem, not the person.** In the wise words of Gottman, this is the strategy of *complaining vs. criticizing*. **Criticism is the first of the Four Horsemen** that can ride into a relationship, marking end times. Criticism attacks a partner's character instead of the problem and will likely elicit **Defensiveness—the second Horseman.**

Criticism sounds like, "Geez, you're such a slob! Your stuff is spread out all over the room and I don't have anywhere to sit!" I can promise if that's how you start out, your partner will shift their attention to the insult and miss your point. On the other hand, a complaint attacks the problem. A complaint in this example sounds like, "I'm having a hard time finding a place to sit in here. Could you clear up some of your things so I can join you?" Because criticism attacks character, contempt is automatically implied. **Contempt is the third Horseman** and the one that is considered the most toxic in a relationship because it communicates disgust for the other person. It's like poison in the water system in your house—it's terrible for everyone.

3. **Avoid using generalization and/or exaggeration, such as "always" and "never."** This is relatively simple to master once you begin to catch yourself using these two words. You could turn it into a game with yourself on your way to being a more effective communicator. Similar to criticism, *always and never* elicit a defensive response and draws out the inner-attorney in most people. It generally goes something like this: "You *always* do [this one thing]." ... Or, "Well, actually, there was that one time back in April two years ago when I didn't do [that thing]." Aaand ... off they go. Same thing with *never*; it ends up as another round of the accuse-and-defend debate one would hear in a court of law.

4. **Stick to the topic and the here and now.** If you want to completely derail an argument, use the "Kitchen Sink Strategy." It's a pile-on technique in which you start with one problem and then add every beef you have with your partner. Maybe you've been storing them up for a while. Then you drag out the relationship history book and dump out those old hurts too. These built-up resentments begin to pour out, deflecting from the problem at hand. It can overwhelm your partner, both of you get into a high

state of arousal, and nothing gets solved. If there are unresolved hurts and lack of forgiveness, get some professional help.

5. **Listen without interrupting and hear the other person.**
People often laugh when I suggest this. Of course it seems obvious, but many experts in communication note that listeners spend more time creating a response in their head than really listening. I would estimate that couples in conflict are probably far WORSE than the average listener. But WHY?

Couples often argue over the day-to-day mundane things, like dishes, laundry, clutter, money, parenting styles, leisure activities, television. You name it. These fights tend to occur when one person's agenda is not aligned with the other person's expectations. At times like this, all listening stops and high-school debate training kicks in. Couples forget that they are on the same team and it is a face-off. But what if they envisioned themselves as being on the same side and facing the problem together, rather than turning on each other and trying to win? I believe the outcome would be completely different. It's worthwhile to ask yourself, "What about this is so important to my partner? Can I give a bit?"

I hate to tell you this but if you are interrupting your partner, you are not listening or truly hearing. While this should be obvious, many interrupters don't recognize they are doing it. It's a bad habit. As one or both partners become increasingly upset, the entire conversation speeds up—as much as anything because neither person feels heard. The real key to effective listening and hearing is to slow down the entire process. Only when each partner feels heard and understood can the real work of negotiation begin.

6. **Manage your emotions—soothe yourself and your partner.**
When we get upset, our nervous system kicks into overdrive. Most people recognize this as the Fight, Flight, or Freeze response.

I call it the "Squirrel Dilemma." You know how they run out in front of your car, turn and see you coming, then twitch back and forth in indecision? Well, let me tell you what is happening in that squirrel's tiny brain: not much! Sadly, we are a lot like those panicky squirrels—we simply cannot think when we get highly aroused. We cannot take in new information accurately and we sure cannot creatively problem-solve. What if, instead, you took your partner's hand or reassured them? What if you took a deep breath and reassured yourself inside? What if you said, aloud or to yourself, "we're on the same side here"? With practice, these could lead to very different discussions.

7. **Use time-outs and don't leave unless you say, "I'll be back."** One way to stay calm is to utilize time-outs. Just like a kid we put in time out when they are having a melt-down, it is a good strategy to settle ourselves so we can reflect on what is really important, and figure out if we need to apologize. Once our heart rates exceed 90 beats per minute, getting back into a normal range generally takes about 20 minutes. If we remain in the fray, we will not likely be able to do that. Taking a time out is another way to take personal responsibility.

Unfortunately, when someone leaves the discussion abruptly by walking out, hanging up, or slamming a door, the other partner feels cut-off and can even panic. This will likely escalate the conflict or create a separation. The action of leaving is loud but unclear. Saying that you will be back is a way to express that you value your partner and your relationship. It helps soothe your partner rather than inciting panic.

8. **Watch your non-verbal communication**, such as eye rolling, mocking, distorted facial expressions, yelling, turning your back, or not responding [**Stonewalling is the Fourth Horseman**]. The

rule of human communication is that *you cannot not communicate.* Everything you *don't* say says something. Even not responding. How many times have you said about an interaction, "It's not *what* you said, it's *how* you said it." In the heat of the moment, most people are seldom aware of what is happening in their voices, face, and body. But your partner never misses it.

9. **No violence—physical or verbal.** While this seems apparent to most people, there are some who grew up with this reality in their own families, or who have poor impulse control and lash out in all kinds of violent ways. Violence, in any form, is nothing but contempt. Violence includes, but is not limited to, hitting, pushing, shaking someone, property damage (throwing things or punching walls), name-calling, cursing, loud yelling, or character assassination.

When a relationship has devolved into violence, it is very likely that the end is near. At the very least, most therapists will direct a couple, at least temporarily, to separate if there is physical violence. It is impossible to do repair work if violence is in the relationship as it erodes the basic tenets of conflict management, such as safety, trust, and even a modest degree of respect.

10. **Be honest.** Simple. But not. Being honest doesn't mean that you speak in an unedited, unkind, hurtful manner. This is not reality TV. Rather you must first get honest with yourself about your side of the disagreement. For example, it might be easier to get angry instead of being vulnerable with your partner and saying you feel hurt. Sometimes you might avoid certain conversations in an attempt to protect your partner, but that often backfires. Even loving, diplomatic truths can make it difficult to be honest. But you owe it to yourself and your partner to deal with harsh realities honestly together.

11. **Be open to a solution.** While this sounds obvious, a fight is often a stand-off in which no one is willing to give in. It makes little sense but we all do it. What is happening below the surface of the conflict is the presence of unexpressed desires. People experience these moments as "do or die," unaware they're not willing to compromise. Instead, ask yourself, "Am I coming to this negotiation with an open heart and mind?" Practicing saying "I am open to a solution here" shifts you from a foxhole—dug in to win—to a collaborative position. Fighting with the sole purpose of getting your way is not about finding a solution.

12. **Don't bother after drinking alcohol or any mind-altering substance.** I'll admit that this seems like a "DUH!" but you would be surprised how often this is EXACTLY when couples tend to fight. I once had a couple who had terribly nasty fights and I began to hear a theme of post-party arguments. I asked, "How often do these fights occur after drinking?" They both squared on me like I'd dropped in from the moon, and in unison said, "*Every time.*" Well, now. That's a whole other problem, isn't it?

The problem with alcohol is that it is disinhibitory. No, alcohol is not a truth serum, but rather people are not restrained in what they are willing to say and blurt out whatever crosses their mind. People say all kinds of stupid stuff they don't mean that, when sober, they would choose not to say. The bigger problem is the hurt experienced by the partner on the receiving end of these unkind, intoxicated slurs. Words hurt and people have a difficult time letting go of them or forgiving their partner.

As you practice these 12 fair-fighting rules, bear in mind that many arguments become circular. After a while, most folks return to the points they already made, mostly because they feel unheard and there is no problem-solving taking place. When that happens, it is time to stop. Just stop. Nothing is getting settled when you begin to loop—you're just replaying the same argument. Limit the conflict to 20-30 minutes. Take a time-out. Agree to reconvene later. Get some sleep—most things are more clear the next day anyway. Take some reflection time to see if you can figure out a creative way to tackle the problem later. Ask yourself, "What do I really want? What is so important to my partner?"

Admittedly, this list can appear a bit intimidating. I suggest that you and your partner review these rules together and determine which ones are creating the biggest problems in your relationship. Pick one and treat it like a game. Accept the challenge to catch yourself making these communication errors and practice one of the twelve fair-fighting rules for a month. If you turn it into a fun challenge—like a couch potato to 5K—you'll get your relationship and your conflict in much better shape! We understand the value of training—so train yourself to learn to fight more fairly. One training day at a time.

LOVE Questions for Reflection and Discussion

What are your beliefs about fighting? Where did you learn them?

How easily do you become overwhelmed in a fight or disagreement?

What attitudes do you bring to a conflict? Are you competitive? Cooperative? Compromising? Or do you just want your way? Be honest and creative here.

LOVE Checklist

☐ With your partner pick one fair-fighting rule to practice. Once you've mastered it, pick another one.

☐ If you have an on-going, unresolved fight going on, try daydreaming multiple solutions to the problem. Even be open to things that may seem ridiculous or absurd. Sometimes opening our minds to larger ideas yields a not-yet-thought-of solution.

☐ Practice saying "yes" first to your partner's solutions.

LOVE Resources

● *Everybody Fights, So Why Not Get Better at It?* by Penn and Kim Holderness (Audiobook only)

● *Non-violent communication: A Language of Life*, by Marshall B. Rosenberg

● There are thousands of online resources. Google "Fair Fighting" and scroll away!!

Notes:

Just as despair can come to one only from other beings, hope, too, can be given to one only by other human beings.

—Elie Wiesel

Soothe Each Other

by *Amy*

It could have been so much worse. My husband and I were teetering on that place where the conversation could have taken a turn down a slippery slope into a fight in an instant.

It was late on a Sunday morning and we were out on a walk when my phone rang. My Dad had been admitted to ICU the night before and I was waiting for news. It was my sister telling me how bad things were.

"Do you think this is a marathon or a sprint?" I asked, stating that if it was going to be a marathon I would come later in the week. "I think it's a sprint. I think this might be the end," she said through tears. "Okay. Nick is here beside me. Let me talk with him and I will call you right back."

We turned a corner and headed for home, talking about what would be the best thing to do. Should I go without him? Wait another day and see if Dad stabilized? Nick was worried about jury duty and we were both concerned about some work and volunteer commitments. We were trying to figure out the details but we were in a state of anxiety. Our voices got more tense and the conversation more pressured. I was trying to manage my own anxiety and his. It wasn't working. I took a deep breath while he was saying something that made things worse. And then I remembered: Soothe him.

Soothe each other. It is a skill that John Gottman says "Marriage Masters" know how to do and "Marriage Disasters" fail at frequently. The prerequisite skill is to be able to regulate your own emotions during conflict or ordeals. We call this self-soothing. Of course we are responsible for our own emotions and reactions. But if you want to be a relationship master, then you learn to soothe the other person when you see their emotional state rise. Sometimes this is also called a repair attempt. You can watch a video of Gottman talking about this on YouTube here: https://bit.ly/3ipUIO5.

I took Nick's hand as we walked. I said to him, "Honey, there has to be an emergency exception for jury duty. There has to be. People get sick, get in car accidents, and die. There has to be a phone number on your form that allows you to call in." He was not soothed. His mind was racing. It was "Yes, but …" for a few more sentences. Then he took a deep breath and we walked a block in silence. Then he tried to soothe me. "Okay. What do you need? I will do whatever you need me to do. I want you to know that." I took a deep breath. We both already had difficult memories around parents' deaths. "Thank you. I know I need to go. But I want you to think very carefully about what your needs are right now. My dad is as much a dad to you as your own step-dad. He tells you all the time you are his son and you always agree. I don't want you to have regrets. I want you to feel good and confident about your own decision." And he took a breath. And our voices softened, and we walked hand-in-hand as we made a plan to leave together as soon as we got home.

Let me assure you, we have not always been good at this. Truth is we have been marriage disasters at several points in our marriage, once to the point of a separation. We are written up in a textbook for marriage and family therapists as a case study (I am not kidding. Our names are disguised to protect us so you won't be able to find us through a search. But trust me, the naked and embarrassing truth is out there for anyone to find.). Any marital failure is the result of many things going badly, and we had many things going badly at different times in our marriage. But hard work (translation: good therapy), deep and active faith lives, vulnerability, true love, good times, the best friends and family, and pure grit has kept us working at this thing we call marriage, and we have come out as a graced and lucky long-term married couple. I wish we had learned some of the skills Rhea and I are sharing with you earlier in our marriage.

Back to soothing each other. It is counter-intuitive, isn't it? When you're having a fight or a disagreement, you want to win, don't you? I always did, and sometimes still do. When we argued in my child-hood home, we argued to win. Not to understand. But now I often ask myself this important question: Do I want to be right or do I want to be in a relationship? Other important questions I've discovered along the way include: Can I listen with sincerity to understand where my partner is coming from? Do I get him? Am I curious enough to ask the right questions to find out what she is really trying to say? Do I know how to soothe my partner?

Soothing your partner is a form of reverse conditioning. If you have a repeated experience of being soothed by your partner, you stop seeing them as a source of anxiety and instead, you associate them with feeling relaxed. There is a release of oxytocin and an automatic increase in the positivity of your marriage. And isn't that what we all want at the end of the day—a peaceful, positive relationship?

So ask your partner what soothes them, if you don't know. Is touch helpful? A quick back rub, taking their hand, or a short kiss might change the tone of a relationship. Does your partner enjoy a little humor? A quick inside joke? Perhaps silence works. Or certain types of music. Or a guided meditation. The way another is soothed is as individual as the person.

We all need to learn to soothe each other. We get nowhere when we are anxious, flooded, and on the battlefield determined to win. Yes, this is an advanced relationship skill. And yes, I believe you can learn it. Soothe yourself. And then soothe the other. It works. It has the potential to turn the messy into marvelous.

LOVE Questions for Reflection and Discussion

How do you soothe yourself during difficult times? What works? A bath? A few deep breaths? Listening to music? Some time alone?

Do you know what would soothe your partner? Touch? Does humor break the tension? A willing attitude? Compromise?

What are some known triggers that agitate you or your partner? How do you navigate those? What does compromise look like if these triggers are unavoidable?

LOVE Checklist

☐ Begin practicing an awareness of your arousal levels. You might even give yourself a rating. For instance, if you come home from work and you are already agitated, say a 7 on a scale of 1-10, practice doing something to lower your level of arousal. This might mean taking a shower, petting the dog, taking a walk, or practicing a few breathing techniques.

☐ Be preventative. If you know you have a stressful time ahead, either for you individually or for your partner, make plans to ease the stress and soothe the senses. You can take things off the to-do list (this week we are going to order food rather than try to shop and cook), you can plan quiet activities, you can practice letting go of perfectionistic demands or standards, etc.

☐ Practice clear, responsible communication. When you are not okay, or you see that your partner is not okay, make a point to slow down the interaction and practice responsible communication (use "I-statements"). Practice active listening and don't take things personal.

LOVE Resources

- *The New Rules of Marriage*, by Terrance Real

- Download a meditation app and begin a daily practice. Popular ones include, Headspace, Calm, Aura, Kardia, and Simple Habit.

Notes:

If you dance close enough with your partner, you're going to step on each other's toes.

—Rhea Merck

Learn to Apologize

by *Rhea*

If learning how to fight fair is hard, then learning how to make a good apology may be the hardest skill of all. It is so rare that when I recently heard it on the TV show *Castle*, I rewound immediately to hear it again. Castle to Beckett, "I'm sorry. What I did was wrong. I violated your trust. I opened old wounds and I did not respect your wishes. And if we're not going to see each other again, then you deserve to know I'm very, very sorry." He turns and walks away, asking her for nothing in return (*Castle*: Season 2, Episode 1: *Deep in Death*).

With ten years in the rearview mirror, I can now see clearly that the lack of apology in my marriage was a critical issue. I was divorced after a relatively long marriage of almost 27 years. Early on, I had a nagging intuition that our pattern of not working through conflicts— not sharing moments of apology and forgiveness—was quite possibly indicative of a greater problem. I'm sure I did the female-trained thing which was to apologize for more than my own behavior. I said I was sorry because I wanted to make things better and/or I wanted the problem to go away. Like so many people, I am pretty conflict-avoidant and I'm sure I was willing to do whatever it took to smooth things over between us. And that has nothing to do with a genuine apology, forgiveness, or reconciliation.

The art of a good apology is the repair work in a relationship. It's obvious that if we wreck something or damage something we own, we fix it. If we wreck our car, we repair it. If a tree falls on our house, we rebuild. Why in the world would we not put as much energy into repairing the relationship that maintains our home and family?

When there is blame and shame, there can be no healing. —Laura Dodson

So what prevents us from being able to effectively clean up our messes? Sometimes, we simply did not learn it in our homes growing up. And then there is shame. Shame is about **who you are,** whereas guilt is about **what you did.** Shame complicates an apology because it is no longer about what you did but about your character. That is hard to accept. And, sometimes it IS about who you are ... the worst of yourself. The antidote is to recognize those shadow parts of yourself: "I cheated on my partner—**I am someone who has it in me to be unfaithful.**" It takes tremendous humility to own those parts of yourself that you don't like so much. Without embracing ALL of who you are and what you're capable of, that stuff just leaks back out and it's hard to make any lasting changes.

I later watched this process play out differently in my life when my midlife boyfriend dramatically overstated something and carelessly handled an issue between us. It hit one of my relational raw spots. Feeling blindsided and triggered, I had a swift and painful reaction to what I experienced as an emotional betrayal and set a firm boundary for this hurtful episode. I actually broke up with him. In the weeks that followed, he did his best to understand my pain and how he'd misstepped. He offered a heartfelt apology, many times, and we had a number of deeply honest conversations to work through the emotions and how the misunderstanding happened. He generously attempted to soothe my feelings but I was having a hard time reengaging and moving forward.

Unexpectedly, I shifted from my stuck place when we ran into friends who knew nothing of the struggle or our brief break-up. When they asked us about something related to "The Big Upset," he immediately stated emphatically, "I totally screwed up." Then he turned to me and asked if he could share the whole story with them. Yes. Yes, you can. He proceeded to admit, "I really messed up. I said something that was not thoughtful or accurate and I really hurt her." He went on to share exactly what he'd said to me, which elicited "shock and awe" expressions from both of them. He handled their admonitions about his choice of words non-defensively and took complete responsibility for the problem, even though it was arguable that my reaction was a bit extreme. He then shared with them how regretful he was about his overstated and misplaced feelings and how much he cherished and loved me.

As we walked away, another layer of the hurt and my own stubbornness to protect my heart began to melt away. I began to see a ray of hope in the heartbroken fog I'd been experiencing and realized that I could work through my hurt feelings and get past this event.

What did he do that was so important? He:

1. took full responsibility.
2. demonstrated his awareness of the pain he caused.
3. did not protect himself or his ego by hiding his mistake from our friends.
4. practiced humility and was actively engaged in holding himself accountable.
5. he took on the transfer of vigilance by sharing with others and not having me be responsible for the story. If I'd told the story, it might have appeared I was shaming him. Because he owned the story, he shared his vulnerability and demonstrated courage.

In her book, *How Can I Forgive You?*, psychologist Janis Abrahms Spring calls this a "Good Apology" in the process of genuine forgiveness, as opposed to cheap forgiveness. She defines cheap forgiveness as a "quick and easy pardon with no processing of emotion and no coming to terms with the injury." You know this is happening when the hurt party simply says, "It's okay," or, "Don't worry about it." Similarly, a cheap apology is an effort to move on quickly and not experience tough emotions like regret or guilt. This is best characterized in three hurried words, "Sorry, sorry, sorry." When someone attempts to apologize in that way, they are really asking you to sweep the matter under the rug and pretend it didn't happen. If more direct and honest, they might as well yell, "Just get over it already!" This is the easiest way to avoid responsibility, to not make the effort to understand how the betrayal happened, and to move on without true healing.

Like repairing the house or the car, this reconciliation process takes time. In big betrayals, like an affair, I use the metaphor of **sleeping on the floor at the foot of the bed for a year.** I got this idea from a *Ladies' Home Journal* column in the 1970s called, *Can This Marriage Be Saved?*, in response to a husband confessing an affair. As a part of his reparation and dedication to his wife, he said that he slept on the floor at the foot of the bed for a year. As with this man, the offending party must be willing to humble themselves in the process of amends, and to demonstrate their willingness to put the work in to repair the offense. The bigger the transgression, the longer it may take to soothe the pain of the hurt party. The wrong-doer must be dedicated to stay the course, to demonstrate their willingness to repair the relationship.

In her book, *Why Won't You Apologize?*, psychotherapist and author Harriet Lerner states that it takes great courage to open up a conversation about a past hurt and to offer a true apology. There are no guarantees on how it will be received nor how it will turn out. But I would suggest that if we truly love someone, we have already agreed to care for one another. If we have done wrong, as a person with integrity, we need to own it. In the end, we will feel comforted and more confident because of our efforts to do the right thing.

How to Make a Good Apology

1. **Apologize for your own behavior.** If you stepped on your partner's toes, you wouldn't say, "I'm so sorry your foot got underneath mine." Well, maybe you could say that but that is NOT an apology—it is blaming the victim. Take responsibility for yourself and your part in the dance. Be direct about what you did rather than hiding your own responsibility. "I am sorry that I yelled at you for that thing," is much more clear and responsible than, "I'm sorry you got upset with what I said."

2. **Take responsibility for the specific hurt(s) you caused.** And not just, "Sorry I hurt your feelings," which is rather minimizing, but, "I know that's a sensitive topic for you and I was callous." What we often hear is, "I'm sorry you felt offended by what happened." You are NOT apologizing for your own behavior but rather offering a pseudo-apology for how the hurt party experienced the betrayal. The implied message is, "You're obviously sensitive and wrong." Taking responsibility may include what you learned from the experience: "I realized that when I feel defensive I go on the attack. I lashed out at you and that was wrong of me."

3. **Make the apology deep and meaningful.** You must be able to show that it is important to you to repair the rift and the pain you caused. "I know I have hurt you and damaged our relationship. I want to make this right and make it up to you." Clear remorse and true behavioral change helps your partner feel understood. It is a demonstration of empathy in action. To show your partner

that you are willing to do what it takes to make things right proves that you are invested in healing. A deep apology removes any question that you are working to save your own image or ego due to your own actions, and places the care for the other person and the relationship front and center.

4. **Make your apology "clean."** You should only attend to the agenda of the apology. Do not defend. Do not problem-solve. Do not say "but." When the word "but" appears in the middle of the sentence, it negates whatever came before it: "I'm sorry for saying that hateful thing *but* you were being such a jerk!" **Be careful that your own emotions don't clutter the agenda of the apology.** While you may certainly be distressed and full of feelings, a big demonstration of your emotions may shut down the process by shifting the attention to you. The hurt party may then begin to feel like they need to take care of you. Remember the goal of the apology is to address the emotions of the hurt party.

5. **Attend to the business of the apology only.** Problem-solving and the circumstances around the betrayal are for another conversation. When these are embedded in the apology, the process is derailed and the focus can shift away from the pain that was caused. Regardless of intent—*but of course, I didn't mean to hurt you*—the consequences of the action are not to be diminished. It is rare that we intend to hurt our partner, so our intentions are not really relevant in this particular conversation.

6. **Make it right.** *Actions speak louder than words* and *talk is cheap.* To offer an apology without offering a remediative action falls short of the mark. Think of something simple and obvious: If you order something and the order is wrong and all the company offers is "We're so sorry" without correcting the order, you would be incensed. You would never do business with them again. An emotion without action falls short of the goal.

7. **Apologize as often as you or your partner need.** There are times when the hurt runs deep and the repair work takes a while to complete. In the situation with my partner mentioned earlier, he needed to repeat the apology, getting to a deeper layer with each profession, "I am so sorry that I threw off our whole plan on where we were going together. I hate that I hurt you with such a thoughtless comment. I hope you can forgive me. I want us to get back on track." I was not going to push the issue but I do confess that each heartfelt expression of regret was like a few more shovels of dirt back in the hole he dug. In the end, healing takes time and effort.

If you make a mess, get out your mop and broom and clean it up. —Virginia Satir

A good, genuine apology can go a long way in repairing a messy relationship breach and reestablishing trust and respect. It contributes to our love and care for our partner. It is even a way we love ourselves as a vital person in the relationship. A good apology helps us build competence as a person who takes responsibility for our actions and the course of our lives. It is a skill that extends to our parents, siblings, children, friends, and beyond.

LOVE Questions for Reflection and Discussion

How were you taught to apologize? How was it modeled in your home?

What is the hardest apology you have ever had to make? What made it so?

From the list above, what do you do well? What is hardest for you?

LOVE Checklist

☐ Have a conversation with your partner about how you as a couple take care of old hurts and betrayals.

☐ Pick an area of apologizing that you could brush up on. Intentionally work on it.

☐ Using a simple example, something that is not too emotionally heavy, practice making a good apology to your partner.

LOVE Resources

How Can I Forgive You? The Courage to Forgive, the Freedom Not to Have To, by Janis Abrahms Spring

Why Won't You Apologize? Healing Big Betrayals and Everyday Hurts, by Harriet Lerner

Podcast: *Unlocking Us* by Brené Brown with Harriet Lerner, *I'm Sorry: How to apologize and why it matters* (2 episodes, May 2020, available on Spotify)

Notes:

This is so much fun! This is what makes an ordinary house your home.

Now is when your house becomes uniquely yours.

The tile patterns, the paint colors, the furniture choices, the aesthetic of it all comes into focus and there is no mistaking that this is yours.

Every partnership has a way of expressing itself as a work of art.

It is a creative collaboration, a labor of love, a beautiful sanctuary, a place of respite. May it be so with yours.

In my community we spend most of our time doing three things: Preparing for ritual, participating in rituals, and recovering from rituals.

—Malidoma Somé, in a speech given at Kanuga Camp and
   Conference Center, 2001

Create Rituals

by *Amy*

When the busyness of daily life is all you can think about, it is hard to imagine making time to create rituals. I want to encourage you, though, as good rituals are the things that can bring beauty, joy, and meaning to a marriage.

If you do not resonate with this word—*ritual*— and wonder what it has to do with healthy love relationships, it might be because our culture has become skeptical of rituals and many of us have not had the opportunity to participate in life-giving rituals. For the purpose of this book, I will define **rituals as symbolic acts designed to open our senses, our hearts, and our imaginations.** Like good poetry or art, **a good ritual suspends ordinary time for a moment and puts our hearts front and center while our egos and thinking selves take a back seat.** A proper ritual should give us something to ponder because it asks questions and offers answers to some of the big "why" issues in life.

In the context of relationships, we might ask, **"Why do we have rituals like marriage ceremonies to confirm our unions?"** Because a relationship deserves to be meticulously and reverently honored. Because we want to publicly announce our intentions in this relationship. Because we might believe there is something at work in this relationship that is a mystery larger than we can even imagine, and we might just open up to that and see what happens. Because we desire the support of our community of friends and family in this difficult and messy endeavor of seeking to love each other.

Historically, rituals were commodities of religious establishments. Baptisms, brises, confirmations, bar mitzvahs, weddings, funerals, and weekly worship were attended by the whole community. These rituals were and still are meant to be so much more than perfunctory. They are meant to change us. A good ritual connects us to ourselves, to others, and, if we so believe, to something bigger than we are. In that it is a symbolic act, it should engage our imaginations and our creativity. **Rituals remind us of what is important, what lasts, and what matters.** And when life is messy, which it always is, a good ritual can surround us, embrace us, and give us something to lean into.

Many couples have daily habits, which are also important in relationships. Some healthy daily habits for a relationship may include agreed upon ways of leaving and greeting each other, remembering to stay in touch during the day, a meal always eaten together, or the daily check-in about work or the kids. These things matter, but they are not rituals.

There can be many elements in rituals, often with specific symbolism: music, spoken words, objects, and natural elements like fire and water. During times of transition in relationships, like moving, having children, or the deaths of parents or grandparents, a ritual may help honor and mark the shift, allowing for integration of intense thoughts and feelings. Developmental changes like midlife, menopause, or andropause can be natural times for a ritual. Bridging the gap between the past and the future—helping us honor who we were, who we are now, and where we are going next—a ritual allows a relationship to observe and honor the rhythms of life.

The natural world gives us tips and instructions for the rhythms of our own lives. Rites of passage, a term most of us are familiar with, can be witnessed in nature and we can take our cues from being keen observers. There are seasons of dormancy, seasons of budding, seasons of blooming, and seasons of fading. These seasons can be seen in our own relationships and we can create rituals around these seasons. Engagements and early marriages are seasons of budding and blooming. Midlife can feel dormant, which for some is anxiety producing. Rather than trust the new life that will emerge, we reach for something that feels new and exciting again. A good midlife ritual could help with this transition. In Skill No. 19 *(Support and Encourage Each Other's Spiritual Journey)*, I talk about my husband's yearly ritual of the sweat lodge. This ritual was an important part of creating meaning in midlife for him.

Let me tell you a story. Many years ago I saw a 20-year-old who was suffering with anxiety. As part of my evaluation, I was taking a detailed history of her childhood, looking for biological/genetic markers, developmental markers, and traumatic events that might be contributing to her anxiety. I clearly remember her description of her parents' marriage. Wedding anniversaries and birthdays were rarely celebrated, meaningful gifts were not exchanged, and a general lack of connectivity existed. She looked sad as she described this to me, and I asked her about her emotions. She teared up and said she didn't understand why they didn't create any rituals (her word) to make their marriage special. Her parents are now divorced.

I do not know all of the reasons for this divorce. However, the lack of ritual ways of honoring this marriage points to one reason. Somehow, the power of ritual to sustain us, to encourage us, to remind us, to bring out the best in us, and to actually transform us appeared absent in this marriage. Many healthy couples I know renew their wedding vows every year. This can be a meaningful relationship ritual. Creating house blessings when a new home is rented or purchased can be helpful to a relationship. Rituals to welcome babies into a family and honoring the transition into parenting are powerful ways to help a couple bond around these new roles. I believe if we had cultural rituals around midlife and empty nest transitions we would have fewer people making messy decisions at these times.

In religious traditions of all kinds, there are rituals of confession. The purpose of a good confession is to remind us that we are human, that we make mistakes, that "our shit stinks too" as one of my mentors frequently said, and to assure us that we continue to evolve and that we are still loved and worthy of being in a relationship. In psychological terms, we would call confession the ability to face our own "shadow self," that part of us that we would rather deny than face. **When we learn to confess and to face our shadow, it is easier to be authentic with ourselves and others and to make good apologies to our partners.** However you can confess, it is a ritual that can work wonders in a partnership.

If the rituals in your life have lost their meaning, you have a couple of choices. You can dig deeper into the ones you are familiar with, perhaps through your religious tradition, and find symbolism that speaks to you. Or, you can find new ones. If you have no rituals in your life, consider creating some. The lack of ritual can actually be dangerous. They are so important to our existence, and we are so wired to need rituals of meaning, that children will create them if they don't have meaningful ones being offered. As odd as this might sound, gang initiations are a dark example of the yearning for ritual, for participating in and belonging to something symbolic and bigger.

Our hearts yearn for symbolic ways to understand the hard things in life. And relationships are one of the many hard things in life. So, rituals can be the glue in relationships. Don't forego them. Don't be lazy about them. They are worth the effort. Attend to them with care and thanksgiving for the beauty that is your relationship. Your love deserves them.

LOVE Questions for Reflection and Discussion

In your family, what were the rituals around love and partnership that you witnessed? Celebrations? Renewal of vows? Annual trips? Perhaps even a funeral was a ritual that was meaningful in your memory.

If you have been part of a religious tradition, how have the rituals around relationships shaped you? Are they still meaningful? Have they lost meaning for you?

The quote at the beginning of this skill comes from a person who spent a lifetime engaged in community rituals. How much care do you put into creating rituals for your partnership? How would you invest your time, talent, and treasure in order to create meaningful rituals?

LOVE Checklist

☐ Plan a ritual with your partner. This could be a wedding, it could be a "bringing baby home," or it could be an empty-nest ritual. Choose music that is meaningful to you. Pick objects that carry symbolic meaning. Find or write poetry or lyrics that speak to this time for you.

☐ Pull out photos of your extended families' rituals: weddings, baptisms, bar mitzvahs, big anniversary celebrations, even funerals. Let these photos loosen your memories and talk with each other about those rituals. Who attended? What funny or meaningful stories do you have around that day?

☐ The next time you attend a wedding, pay attention to the symbolic meaning of the day. Take note of the language, the symbols, the words, the readings. Put your imagination and creativity to work as you allow the ritual to connect you to something deeper.

LOVE Resources

The Art of Gathering: How We Meet and Why It Matters, by Priya Parker

The Power of Rituals: Turning Everyday Activities into Soulful Practices, by Casper Ter Kuile

Ritual: Power, Healing, and Community, by Malidoma Patrice Somé

Notes:

You were born with wings: why prefer to crawl through life?

—Rumi

Support and Encourage Each Other's Spiritual Journey

by *Amy*

In addition to being a critical *skill* for a partnership, encouraging and aligning with your partner's spiritual journey might just be the greatest *gift* you can give them.

I am fortunate that my husband and I understood the importance of structuring our marriage in order to support our spiritual lives while we were still fairly young. Some of this revolved around our church life, where having an active, engaged community gave us opportunities to explore our faith journeys as well as to volunteer in meaningful ways. Some of it was outside of that church life, reading books and discussing them with each other and sometimes with our friends. For holidays and birthdays, we gift each other spiritual books and experiences that support and encourage our journeys.

I witnessed a real transformation and healing for my husband after a series of men's retreats he attended in the 1990s, led by an Episcopal priest and two Jungian therapists. During this retreat, the men built a sweat lodge and participated in the ancient Native American ritual of the sweat. The process of literally stripping naked and praying for self and others, of essentially dying to Self in the tent and then being resurrected upon leaving the tent, changed forever the way he allowed himself to be vulnerable and spiritually available.

A spiritual journey does not necessarily mean a religious journey, although it might. **I believe a spiritual journey is the yearning in each of us to create a meaningful life.** Professor Martin Seligman, author of *Learned Optimism (2006), Authentic Happiness (2004),* and *Flourish* (2012), writes and speaks at length about creating a meaningful life. He works specifically in the field of positive psychology and delineates between the pleasant life, the engaged life, and the meaningful life. It turns out through much research that seeking pleasure has almost no impact on life satisfaction. However, people who have meaningful lives report tremendous life satisfaction. A meaningful life has these components. A person:

- knows their signature strengths.
- intentionally designs their life to use those strengths in work, play, friendships, partnerships, and parenting.
- uses those strengths to belong to, and in service of, something larger than they are.

So supporting your partner in creating a meaningful life, remembering that a marriage is a part of what gives one's life meaning, may not be something that brings you or them exquisite pleasure. But it will lead to a better life, a good life, a meaningful life. Pleasure comes and goes, has a rise and a fall. Pleasure also has a habituation effect, meaning that we get used to pleasure and then want more and more of it. Seeking pleasure is a bottomless pit. Seeking meaning, however, satisfies for the long haul. After a meaningful experience, people will report a higher satisfaction with life for days, weeks, months, and even years. It is in the best interest of everybody to find meaning in life, because **meaning creates that sense of serving something bigger than the self, and that creates deep satisfaction.**

Like anything worthwhile, practice matters. Whether you are working on mental resilience, physical fitness, emotional intelligence, or spiritual alignment, having supportive practices will make a difference. Following are a few ways that you can create a container with your partner that will support your spiritual alignment, as well as each other's spiritual journeys.

Continue to clarify your own values and deepen your self-knowledge.

- What are your core beliefs and values?
- What are your signature strengths?
- Are you committed to a particular religion or spiritual community?
- What are your daily/weekly/yearly practices that keep you fed and nurtured spiritually?
- How comfortable are you having hard conversations about existential topics like consciousness, faith, hope, justice?

These questions might be important to ask yourself before you are committed to another person (*Skill No. 1: Choose Your Partner Carefully*). They are certainly critical to ask during the course of a relationship. Don't be afraid if the answers to these questions change over time, because they might! As we grow, our spiritual beliefs and practices evolve as well.

The youngest child of good friends of ours joined us for dinner one night with her new fiancé. I asked how they met and found out they had met on a dating app. A little surprised because of all the horror stories I have heard over the years, I asked how they, two perfectly lovely people, managed to find each other on this app. She answered by sharing that her profile read, "I love Jesus. Do not even respond to me if this is a problem for you." That cut out a whole lot of prospective suitors. But this man who responded to her had a deep devotion to his faith as well, and they were already supporting each other's spiritual journeys. In the course of just a couple of hours of being with them, I could tell that their relationship had a solid foundation.

Design daily, weekly, and other regular spiritual practices.

Many couples share a daily time of meditation or devotion. This may be a short daily devotion received in their inbox, a time of sitting and meditating or praying together, a reading from sacred texts, or even reading the same book together. The focus is on the "something bigger than each of us individually," and is about listening for meaning and purpose in life and in marriage.

Weekly practices may involve attending a religious service together or keeping a sabbath day of rest each week. Some couples I know are members of a small group of some kind. These groups may eat or study together, or they may just be people with whom there is a shared concern for each other and a safe place to come with joys and sorrows.

My husband and I have attended a retreat together for the past seven years. AwakeningSoul is a retreat designed for sanctuary, sustenance, and inspiration. We have found the three days away together, listening to wonderful music, hearing inspiring speakers, and having a chance to more deeply connect with each other, strengthens not only our individual journeys, but also strengthens us as a couple.

Have deep conversations.

Different from the hard conversations of Skill No. 13, these conversations revolve around a sincere desire to know that state of your partner's soul. It is so easy and natural after a busy day at work and a full life at home to crash in front of your favorite Netflix series or grab that novel you have been wanting to finish. **These conversations take intentionality and time, but they are so important to the sense of spiritual connection that a couple feels.** Consider a few of these questions:

- How is your soul these days?
- What is bringing you joy?
- What is draining you?
- How are you processing what is going on in the world?
- How are you grieving, or celebrating, or integrating, the hard experiences in your life?

Make time for sexual intimacy, or as Skill No. 12 suggests, Do It.

Intimacy can be like glue in a marriage. When practiced intentionally and with reverence, sexual intimacy can also bridge the spiritual and physical realms. It is not counterintuitive to say that a good sex life is a part of a supportive spiritual life. Many mentors have helped me to understand that **spirituality, sexuality, and creativity all come from the same place in a person.** When we attend to one, we are often attending to all three.

I want to leave you with a thought and an image. Your marriage or committed partnership is its own entity. You are an entity, your partner is an entity, and the marriage is an entity of its own. It needs nurturance, support, safety, encouragement, and attention. Without these things, it will die, even if the two people live on. I like to think of a marriage as an evolving piece of art. If we were walking down the street with our partners and there was an image that surrounded us that represented our marriage, what would it be? What color would your partnership be? What shape? How rigid? Fluid? How connected? How much space? Would it be connected to something larger than itself?

By encouraging and aligning with your partner's spiritual journey, you are creating a relationship that will have deep roots, resilience for the hard times, the capacity to evolve and expand, and the possibility of creating a truly meaningful—and marvelous—life.

LOVE Questions for Reflection and Discussion

How would you define your "spiritual journey"? Would you be able to describe it to your partner? In other words, how would you describe the meaning of life to yourself or another?

What do you do to take care of your own spiritual journey?

Could you have a conversation with your partner about the five questions listed on page 189? Why or why not? Do you think it is important?

LOVE Checklist

☐ Make time in your life on a daily, weekly, monthly, and yearly basis for spiritual journeying. This can be as simple as a meditation practice, a journaling practice, group book studies or Bible studies, short retreats, reading, or longer periods of immersion.

☐ Encourage your partner to do the same. Honor the requests made to have time apart for this purpose.

☐ If it feels safe, share your discoveries and growth with your partner.

LOVE Resources

The Enneagram is a personality and spiritual tool that is helpful to many couples I know. There are many ways to engage with the Enneagram, and so many resources available now there is no need to list them all. If you are curious, I would start at the website, enneagraminstitute.com and take the RHETI (Riso-Hudson Enneagram Typology Indicator) test. For a small price you get detailed feedback. Whenever I encourage couples to look into this, there is often a big "thank you" and an "I wish we had known about this sooner."

The Wisdom of the Enneagram, by Don Richard Riso and Russ Hudson

The Enneagram in Love and Work: Understanding Your Business and Intimate Relationships, by Helen Palmer

Podcasts galore on the Enneagram. I like Ian Cron's *Typology*, and Suzanne Stabile's *The Enneagram Journey*.

The Road Back to You: An Enneagram Journey to Self-Discovery, by Cron and Stabile

The Path between Us: An Enneagram Journey to Healthy Relationships, by Suzanne Stabile

The Complete Enneagram: 27 Paths to Greater Self-Knowledge, by Beatrice Chestnut

Virtues Cards, by virtuesproject.com. These are one of my favorite ways to have conversations about virtues and how we practice them. A deck of virtues cards contains 100 cards, each with a separate virtue on it— think patience, kindness, honesty, resilience, compassion, etc. Each card explains the virtue, suggests a way of practicing the virtue, and also includes a quote about the topic. Pulling a card a week to have as conversation with your partner is a good idea.

The Family Virtues Guide: Simple Ways To Bring Out The Best In Children And In Ourselves, by Linda Kavelin Popov. Written by the same woman who began the virtues project, this book is for use by families with children (maybe beginning with early elementary school) and devotes a few pages to each virtue with ways of developing that virtue.

Strengthsfinders 2.0, by Tom Rath. Buy the book and get a free code to take the test on gallup.com. If you want to know how to think about your strengths and how to bring them into your relationship, this might be a good place to start.

The course of true love never did run smooth.

—Lysander, in William Shakespeare's *A Midsummer
   Night's Dream*

Life Partnering Skill No. 20

Keep It Up

by *Rhea*

If you're on your way to mastery as a life-partner builder, remember that you're going to be living here—in this relationship—for a long time. You will be required to do maintenance and updating over time. Keep it up!

"Do you mind if I ask, are you married?" asked my client, a high energy, very successful professional whose similarly well-educated spouse had quit their job a year into the marriage, floundering and largely unemployed ever since.

"Well, I'm divorced. But I had a pretty long-term marriage, almost 27 years."

"Oh. Well then you know. We've been married ten years and it's just kind of flat—you know, the same ole, same ole. Nothing exciting. That's just the way it is in a marriage, isn't it?"

I would love to tell you that this is a rare exchange in my office, but it isn't. Not only was the marriage flat, but this client's life was also quite flat. Child-free by choice, they were not distracted by little people in their home. My client had been very focused on career advancement and professional activities that were described as "a real adrenaline rush." The left-at-home partner felt increasingly isolated, lonely, and

195

lost. A perfect couple-concocted recipe for distance. So I asked my client some of the following:

- What did you enjoy in your partner early on?
- How did you spend your time together in the early years?
- Do you bring energy home or leave that at the office?
- Do you assume you know everything there is to know about your partner?
- Are you avoiding facing the disappointment you feel about your partner's struggle?
- Are you avoiding your partner?
- Do you create adventures together?
- Do you intentionally touch one another?
- Do you still share long kisses?
- Do you look in each other's eyes?
- Do you share more negative emotions than positive ones?
- How often do you laugh together *(Skill No. 11)?*

As discussed in Skill No. 2 *(Be Your Best Self)*, complacency is hard to fight. Routine is the enemy of novelty, so it's easy for interest to wane. Our brains love efficiency and as a result, we become lazy in our efforts. We get tired at work and we have nothing left when we come home. We get distracted with low-energy activities (like TV, video games, or reading—not that there's anything wrong with any of these) at the end of a long day. But with this as our default setting, we are not bringing anything home to the relationship, and it will sag as a result.

It is a fact that marriages, and any long-term, committed, romantic relationships, will wax and wane over time. But keep in mind, there are seasons to all things in life. The key is whether we feed, water, nourish, and prune (as needed), our relationships. Or do we throw them out on the porch and expect them to thrive? Even the most carefully tended blooming plants die back, rest, and then bloom again. It is important to be realistic and to know that there are stages in all love relationships.

In her book, *The Truth About Love*, Dr. Pat Love discusses these relationship stages. She says that the "Infatuation" stage brings you together and will be necessarily followed by the "Post-Rapture" stage, which shows you reality. A couple finds their way out of low spots by engaging in the "Discovery" stage, and the "Connection" stage knits you back together at a deeper level of love. According to Dr. Love (how convenient, huh?!), we cycle through these stages during the long course of our coupled life. It strikes me that both *Discover* and *Connect* are action words, whereas *Infatuation* and *Post-Rapture* are awareness words. **The path out of complacency and boredom is clearly marked by taking action.**

The things we did early on in a relationship are still important to maintain—not simply to attain—the partnership. When you were first dating, you probably did these four things easily and it's worthwhile to revisit them regularly.

1. **Remain curious.** Learn to ask good questions. You *think* you know what your partner thinks or feels or believes, but try asking anyway. And then ask the next question. Learn the fine art of probing for more: *What do you think drives that? Tell me how you formed that belief. How long have you felt that way? What shaped that idea? How far back do you remember feeling that?* What would happen in our relationships if we tried to learn something new about our partner every day?

2. **Touch each other.** Did you know that kissing for six seconds or more releases all those bonding hormones? It also decreases levels of cortisol, the stress hormone. Sex releases even more bonding

hormones (oxytocin and vasopressin), decreases cortisol, and bathes our brains in rewarding dopamine. Touch, specifically in the form of hugging, has been shown to boost the immune system. Touch often. It is the intimacy of this special relationship that sets it apart from most others. Enjoy that unique connection together.

3. **Be intentional.** We put everything on our schedules that is important. But many people stubbornly refuse to "schedule intimacy." Why not? If it's not sanctioned on our schedules, relationship ends up as an afterthought, we run out of steam, our partner ends up in last place, and affection wanes. Sanctioning time together allows you the space you need to nurture more connection. No time means no opportunity.

4. **Create adventures.** No, not skydiving ... unless that's your thing. Novelty with your partner jump-starts the reward system in your brain and can make your partner look more attractive. Learn something new together. Travel. An adventure might be as simple as taking walks (that you are now scheduling together) in new settings, musing about your environment, discussing recent events, or sharing your hopes and dreams. Now you're connecting!

Like anything we want to be good at, we need to practice, practice, practice. We manage to do these four things early on in our relationship, so why quit now, unless you want to fail? Life is messy enough without hard and expensive break-ups to work through. This short list is not difficult to do and will communicate to your partner that you value them and your relationship together.

I don't often speak publicly about my own divorce because it is not just my story, but that of my whole family and I want to respect their privacy. What I *can* tell you is that my marriage did not die of neglect. Having been married young and so many years, I am often asked, "Well, I guess you just grew apart?" My answer is, "I wish it were that simple." In fact, as the children were leaving the nest, we often discussed what life would look like after 20+ years of raising our daughters. We'd actively and intentionally embarked on rediscovered hobbies and interests we enjoyed together but had not been able to do with the demands of kids at home. I wholeheartedly believe that "growing apart" is repairable. It is actionable. And if both parties are focused on that goal, it is achievable.

To love someone is a decision that we make each and every day. I believe the key to a long-term relationship can be summed in two words: **Stay connected.** Whatever that means for you and at whatever level of effort it takes. It is a decision. Every day. *Keep It Up!*

LOVE Questions for Reflection and Discussion

What you nurture grows. So, how do you invest your time, attention, curiosity, and Self with your partner?

When you feel a disconnect or a "flatness" in your relationship, how do you address it?

Many of the tasks and commitments of day-to-day life are mundane. How do you tolerate routine and/or boredom?

LOVE Checklist

☐ Make a list of things that are fun for both of you. Make sure you include things that are easily accessible.

☐ Practice being curious about each other's world and find ways to connect there.

☐ Share with your partner when you feel vulnerable to boredom and disinterest. Make a plan for how to navigate those inevitable droughts.

LOVE Resources

The Truth about Love, by Dr. Pat Love

The Secret to Desire in a Long-term Relationship, TEDSalon, Esther Perel

Mating in Captivity, by Esther Perel

"Come in," she said, *"I'll give you shelter from the storm."*

—Bob Dylan

Epilogue

For Better or for Worse

by *Rhea*

Relationships are at the core of our lives. And our long-term love partnerships, when in their best forms, can provide the sanctuary in which we find joy, meaning, and shelter in the world. We do expect a great deal from our relationships, but if we're realistic, we can live a marvelous life together, sharing the burden of life's inevitable messes.

For better or worse, our primary partnership or marriage shapes the course of our lives. Most of the big decisions we make in life—picking a major in college, grad school, career, buying a house, moving to a new city—can be relatively easy to change. But when a marriage fails, the immediate toll is significant. In many cases, the emotional and financial consequences are long-term. This makes it worth the effort to choose well, bring your best self, and work on improving your relationship skills daily. The best news is that the skills in this book can help you dramatically improve the quality of your love life.

That said, there are times and situations which create a hardship too difficult to overcome. It may be you, or your partner, who loses the motivation and desire to press on together. Other times, there are personal issues so great that the relationship pays too high a price. Divorce is hard, and yet, for some people it is the answer. No judgment here! But if you find yourself back out there in the dating pool again, it is a worthwhile investment for your next relationship to work on your own self and your relationship skills. Maybe you can alleviate future heartbreak.

Relationships are messy and marvelous. But isn't everything that is worthwhile?

Wisdom from Years (237 of them) of Marriage

by *Amy*

Over the holidays, my husband, daughter, and I used to participate in two "ritual" dinner parties. One was affectionately known as "The Night Before The Night Before" (**TNBTNB**), and the other is our New Year's Eve Dinner Extravaganza. (**NYEDE**). I wasn't thinking about the possibility that these occasions would continue for decades, which they both did. One ended after about 20 years when several adult children moved away and too many of us were traveling. And the other is still going strong after what we think is well over 30 years. We didn't keep a record of when things started, so we have relied on memories to come up with the commencement of these long-standing rituals. So, relying on memories, "Okay, we had it at your house when you lived in this neighborhood the first year, because I remember you had just moved in and your youngest one was recovering from chicken pox." These numbers are an approximation, but all participants agree it is a fairly close accounting.

Each year the dinner conversations are lively and intimate, but also surprising because we never know where the conversation will lead. Both events were usually intergenerational, and as the children turned into adults, some brought friends or a significant other to join in. One year, at both parties, the topic turned to the number of years of first marriages that were sitting around the table. That year at **TNBTNB**, we had a cumulative 101 years from four couples in first marriages. At the **NYEDE** we had 136 years of first-marriage experience at the table.

Now this seems like a lot of relationship wisdom to me. So I asked the question: *What do you think are the most important qualities in a lasting marriage?* I have been pondering the answers ever since. As you'll surely notice, many themes from these wise and wonderful responses are also skills in this book! While all of the answers were given and taken seriously, some are funnier than others. They all deserve sharing. Here they are.

Have Respect. This piece of advice came from the wife of the youngest married couple, only two years of marriage underneath them. Already, though, her relational wisdom shined. The research shows repeatedly that respect and trust are the foundation of any marriage. Without these two components, chances of a vibrant, healthy, life-giving marriage are slim.

Compromise. You have to learn to give and take. You have to remember it isn't all about you. In a true compromise, both parties get something and both parties lose something. If you help me with the yard work this morning, I will be able to play nine holes with you this afternoon. You didn't really want to do yard work and I did not really want to golf, but this compromise works because we are both getting something we want.

Have a spouse who travels some, or maybe a lot. Sometimes a little space is a good thing. In marriages when the personalities are very different, or if one person likes a little more space, or if one person loves being on the go, this can be a helpful piece of advice. It is quite sentimental to believe that all married couples want to be together every night of the week. This might be more true after children are grown and more independent, but I can honestly tell you that I kind of crave those nights when I can read magazines in bed and leave them lying all around me and fall asleep, reading, with the light on. I also love being able to come home to deep quiet some nights. No conversation. No noise. And just for the record, this one was not my piece of advice, but I agree!

Have a lot of sex, even when you don't want to. Nearing thirty years of marriage, this advice came from a wise woman. Sex, while not the be-all-end-all of a marriage, is often the glue in married life. And while sex should never be forced, she (and I) believe that it is quite okay to have sex from a giving, generous stance; I don't really feel like it but I know it's important to you and ultimately to us. In sex, we are restating our commitment to somehow mysteriously join each other not only physically but spiritually. **Oh, and it is just plain fun.** And good for your brain. And your body. And your mood. So yeah, have a lot of sex.

Sacrifice/death of self. The man who offered this quality had trouble getting words around what he was trying to say. He was saying things like don't sweat the little stuff, and let things go, and figure out what ditch you really want to die in. And then someone at the table offered the word "sacrifice." And he lit up. "Yes, that's it." And then another woman at the table said, "death of self," to which we, the collective table, said, "Yesssss … perfect." This is little "s" self, like your ego. Death of ego. Death of needing to be right. Death of always getting your way.

Marry your best friend. This advice was given quickly by one of the quieter members at the table of the NYEDE. But he spoke up almost immediately, which to me is a sign that he has integrated this truth into his life. "I married my best friend. That's why we are still married." This has some real heft to it, doesn't it? Why? Because many couples are in what Gay and Katie Hendrix call "entanglements" rather than intimate relationships. In an entanglement, a couple is not truly comfortable together. They are not each other's best friend and so there is often a palpable level of tension. Marrying your best friend prevents being in an entanglement.

Negotiate. Why is being able to negotiate important in a marriage? Each person needs to be able to clearly state his or her point, and this clarity of communication helps develop friendship and understanding. Being able to negotiate means you know your own position and can understand at least a portion of what your partner is saying, even if you don't get the whole thing. Negotiation requires active listening and compromise. This is good for any relationship.

Keep a sense of humor. One of the reasons I married my husband is because he makes me laugh, and he has taught me to laugh more. Marriage can be full of comedy and tragedy, and developing an ironic and comedic eye can be an amazingly constructive and creative endeavor. It is good to be able to laugh, even in the middle of crises. It is good to have the capacity to break up an intense moment with a clear sense of the comedic or the ironic. It has sure helped me in my marriage.

Have fun. *Couples that play together stay together.* Also heard as *Couples that pray together stay together.* Playing and praying are not as far apart as they may seem. Both true play and true spirituality come from the same place in us, that place of intimacy and connection. So having fun is critical to the connection of a marriage. In small ways, dancing in the kitchen, telling jokes, laughing at a movie, playing games together, playing sports together, praying together, or visiting with friends, make sure fun is a part of your marriage.

Create and participate in rituals. If you have read my first book, *Moment to Moment: The Transformative Power of Everyday Life,* you already know that one of my favorite ways to spend time is around a dinner table with good friends and good food. Over the years, rituals like the ones I am describing, TNBTNB and the NYEDE, have become bedrocks of our married life. I am honored to be a part of these rituals. They give life meaning on so many levels. There are many other rituals in which we participate, because I believe rituals bind us together in ever-deepening ways. Rituals give meaning to life. They speak to the mysterious nature of this life we are trying to live.

Learn to apologize. How most of us hate to apologize! I mean a real apology. An "I'm sorry" without the necessary understanding of how you have hurt the other person can actually make the damage worse. There are components to a good apology. Learn them.

Forgive. I put this quality last on purpose. Married life will not be without hurt and betrayal. Even the best marriages have had their day in the trenches. Learning the process of forgiveness can be key to a lasting marriage. Forgiveness does not mean that you are pretending you weren't hurt. Forgiveness means that you have worked through the issues or events so that they have no power in your life anymore. It's some of the best work you can do for yourself.

So I gift you this wisdom, offered from dear friends at ritual dinner parties: a collective 237 years' worth of first marriages. At the time of this printing, all are still married. Much of this wisdom mirrors the skills in this LOVE guide that you are reading now. May these ideas bless your own life partnership and bring you much to consider.

About the Authors

Dr. Amy Sander Montanez has been in private practice since 1988. She holds a Master's Degree in Counseling from Clemson University and a D.Min. in Spiritual Formation from Graduate Theological Institute. In 2013, Amy's first book, *Moment to Moment: The Transformative Power of Everyday Life,* was awarded Spirituality and Health's Top 100 books of the year. Amy works with all aspects of women's issues, emerging adults, couples and families, and grief. She is known for her work with clergy of all denominations and seminarians. Outside of the office she loves to cook and entertain, play the piano, listen to live music, dance, read, and gather with friends and family. Her husband, Nick, and daughter, Maria, are huge sources of joy in her life. amysandermontanez.com

Dr. Rhea Ann Merck has worked in the field of mental health since 1984. She earned her M.S. and Ph.D. in Counseling Psychology from the University of North Texas. Rhea has worked in a variety of clinical settings with adults, emerging adults, teens, couples, and families. Since 1996, she has maintained a private practice in Columbia SC, and is also  employed with the Athletic Department at the University of South Carolina. Previously, as an Instructor in Psychology, she was honored with the UofSC College of Arts and Sciences Undergraduate Teaching Award in 2019–2020. Rhea is the mother of two fine humans, Caitlin and Rebekah. In her free time, she enjoys live music, travel, painting, writing, entertaining, and anything that brings her together with friends and family. ramphd.com

Together they co-author the blog, MessyMarvelous.com Their first book is *LAUNCH: A Guide to Adulting.* Look for them in social media as @messyandmarvelous.

Made in the USA
Middletown, DE
08 July 2023

34749889R00119